Mud
A MILITARY HISTORY

Related Potomac Titles

The Forgotten Soldier—Guy Sajer

Heavy Metal: A Tank Company's Battle to Baghdad—
Jason Conroy with Ron Martz

*Military Geography: For Professionals and
the Public*—John M. Collins

An AUSA Book

Mud
A MILITARY HISTORY

C. E. Wood

Potomac Books, Inc.
Washington, D.C.

Library of Congress Cataloging-in-Publication Data

Wood, C. E. (Clyde Edward)
  Mud : a military history / C. E. Wood.— 1st ed.
     p. cm.
  Includes bibliographical references and index.
  ISBN 1-57488-984-2 (hardcover : alk. paper)
  1. Mud. 2. Military history. I. Title.
  U27.W64 2006
  623—dc22

                                        2005030029

Printed in the United States of America on acid-free paper that
meets the American National Standards Institute Z39-48
Standard.

Potomac Books, Inc.
22841 Quicksilver Drive
Dulles, Virginia 20166

First Edition

10 9 8 7 6 5 4 3 2 1

IN MEMORY

Staff Sergeant M. R. Connor, USMC
Lance Corporal A. O. Garza, USMC
Private First Class M. A. Noline, USMC

January 26, 1991

CONTENTS

PHOTOGRAPHS

ACKNOWLEDGMENTS

The assistance and advice provided by my doctoral committee was indispensable in expanding my dissertation into this book. Consequently, I am indebted to Drs. Lloyd Ambrosius, Parks Coble, Ed Homze, Pete Maslowski, and David Wishart. In addition, my appreciation extends to the various staff members at the U.S. Army Military History Institute and at the National Archives in College Park, Maryland. These hardworking individuals retrieved numerous records and photographs for my benefit. I am grateful as well to my colleagues in the Department of Social Sciences, Drs. Jack Brown, Art DeMatteo, Amy DeWitt, Mike Gherke, Jill Haasch, Mike Smith, and Fred Walborn, who have assisted me in my research and writing. Aiding me in my work were our department secretary, Mrs. Carol Goodrich, and student workers, Ms. Jenny James, Mr. Robinson Lubin, and Ms. Lindsey Taylor. I also wish to thank Dr. Jim Bartholomew who helped me understand the physical properties of mud. Thanks to Don McKeon and the staff at Potomac Books, Inc. for transferring my work into a book for a wider audience.

The most difficult part of my research was finding examples of mud in war, since few authors include mud in their indexes. Several people helped me in my quest by providing bibliographic data and quotes whenever they encountered mud in their reading or research. Thanks to

Drs. William Atwater, Dane Kennedy, Steven Ramold, Gary Trogdon, Chuck Vollan, and Bob Watrel. Also taking the time to read various memoirs were Col. Scott Ayres, Pvt. Clayton Barker, and my uncle, Mr. Jerry Sharp. My mother, Mrs. Kathryn Wood, helped revise the manuscript.

My deepest appreciation goes to my fiancée, Ms. Chandra DeBuse, who read the entire work, offered advice, and provided motivational support despite having no interest in mud or military history.

INTRODUCTION

A lthough combat veterans have long understood mud's significance, combat experience is not a prerequisite for familiarity with mud. Those individuals who have spent most of their adult lives in the military, yet never saw a shot fired during conflict, still know the trials that wet soil brings. The observations of Lt. Gen. E. L. M. Burns, who survived the first and second world wars, stress the importance of mud in military history. In his opinion, the "most lasting impression" he sustained from his experiences in both wars was how much more soldiers could accomplish with good weather, and little to no mud, versus the horrendous struggles for "a few hundred yards through the mud" in such major battles as the Somme and Passchendaele.[1]

This book concentrates on the military history of Europe, Asia, and North America. Mud's impact on military operations in Africa and South America is equally important, but readers will find few references to these areas. Warfare occurred on these two continents, of course, but two things are lacking. First, African warfare does not provide the large number of individual memoirs like those from European, American, and Asian experiences. Second, much of the primary source material available from Africa and South America is not available in English.

The book does not specifically cover mud associated with bodies of water, that is, the mud found in and around the oceans, seas, lakes, rivers, and in such situations as the tidal mudflats at Inchon on the Korean pennisula. Similarly, such materials as dried mud used in buildings and fortifications do not really fit with the concept of mud discussed here.

In researching mud's historical influence, I have given certain periods and regions more attention than others. Most of the evidence comes from the last couple of centuries when a wider variety of weapons and weapon platforms existed than in earlier conflicts. Although the twentieth century saw fewer conflicts in which edged weapons were the primary weapons system, the twentieth century added motorized vehicles and aircraft. These innovations yielded many new encounters with mud, yet modern conflicts still included horses, wagons, edged weapons, and combatants on foot just as wars of the ancient and medieval world did.

No historians, and few geographers, have conducted more than a limited examination of mud's military influences. Among the few books that do credit mud are Patrick O'Sullivan's *Terrain and Tactics*, John Collins's *Military Geography*, and *Battling the Elements*, a collaborative effort led by Harold A. Winters.

Although *Terrain and Tactics* provides a diverse view of military operations, the work concentrates mostly on geographic regions and types of warfare and discusses little about mud. *Military Geography* covers all aspects of physical geography (weather, soils, landforms, and hydrology) and their impact on military operations. Collins's book includes mud as a specific factor on the large and small scale, but except for a few brief examples proving his respective points, he concentrates on mud's significance as a hindrance to mobility. He does not, for example, adequately examine mud's influence on a combatant's health, morale, and endurance.

Battling the Elements is the best work written on mud, using Gen. Ambrose Burnside's Mud March in the American Civil War, Passchendaele from World War I, and World War II's Eastern Front as examples of its influence. Winters explains how mud degraded mobility, but the book is not a history of mud's influence on warfare. Its two chapters on mud are a small section of a work that emphasizes the broad spectrum of military geography and does not explain mud's influence on combatants, animals, and machines.

One of the more important works on mud's influence on military operations was developed in the mid-1950s when the U.S. Army commissioned several studies to determine the environment's effect on military operations. Using recent experiences in the Korean War and operations in World War II's European Theater, these researchers compiled 9,203 cases when units mentioned environmental factors in their after-action reports. Norman Randolph Mason Jr. presented their findings in several tables (Appendix, Table 2 and Table 3). The primary way mud affects military operations is by hindering or countering forward movement. According to Robert Campbell, 95 percent of all reported incidents of mud involved movement.[2]

This book is a general examination of mud's influence on military history. Since the scope of such an endeavor is tremendous, its parameters require definition. First, the primary focus is transitional mud, the kind that arrives and departs without significant warning; hence only one chapter pertains to such permanent geographic features as swamps, marshes, and bogs where mud is a constant. The book breaks down mud's influence in three ways. First, it defines mud and identifies its characteristics and effects and how they hinder combatants, animals, and machines. Second, it discusses how mud's transitory nature influences battlefields and a commander's plans through permanent, seasonal, and random mud. Finally, this book examines how mud affected engineers and a combatant's health, morale, and endurance, and takes a look at how the U.S. military is dealing with mud today.

CHAPTER 1

Mud's Types, Characteristics, and Effects

"No commander in modern warfare can fully understand his battles unless he fully knows his battlefields below, as well as on, the surface."
–Douglas W. Johnson [1]

Any veteran who has dealt with mud understands or has probably told a variation of the following hyperbole, which conveys the magnitude of deep mud. "As we were marching to the front as a relief unit, a comrade's helmet slipped off his head. He poked around in the mud with a stick to find the smelly hat again. Suddenly he discovered a human face. Dumfounded, he asked: 'Gee, how did you get there?' At that, the face said: 'You'll be surprised when you learn that I'm sitting on a horse and riding.'" [2]

John Collins, author of *Military Geography: For Professionals and the Public,* describes one reason why no general or historian has sunk his or her teeth into the impact mud has made on military history. "Commanders, staffs, and subordinates from the highest to the lowest of every armed service need to know how geology and soils affect combat and support operations, but most are bored to tears by those technical subjects." For emphasis, he adds how mud sends "tanks and armored fighting vehicles sliding down slopes like Olympic-class luges."[3] His explanation may help historians understand why mud does not receive the attention it is due.

First, what is mud? Second, in what geographic locations does mud occur readily? Geographic dictionaries such as F. J. Monkhouse's *A Dictionary of Geography* (1970) and W. G. Moore's *A Dictionary of Geography* (1968) have no definition for mud. Another geographic dictionary has this single entry: "an unconsolidated rock of clay-grade often containing much water."[4] Other mud definitions include "a fluid to plastic mixture of clay and/or silt and water" and "mud is simply a mixture of water and small fragments of decomposed rock."[5]

The essential ingredients for making mud are soil and moisture. Soil covers the land from depths as great as several hundred feet to just a few inches, and although soil is essential, mud does not exist without excessive moisture.[6] If the soil component disappears but moisture remains, mud losses its plasticity and becomes dirty water. Lower the soil-moisture ratio and mud reverts to its "normal" state. Remove all moisture from the ground and soil can turn to dust. A soil's parent material and its moisture-holding capabilities also determine mud formation.

Moisture retention in soil depends on the soil's porosity and permeability. Porosity is the total volume of open pore spaces in a material and relates closely to the material's ability to absorb moisture. Permeability is a measure of a material's ability to transmit water; the larger the particle size of a soil, the more easily moisture filters down away from the surface. Farmers cultivate their soil by trying to enhance water's penetration of the soil, and consequently "cultivated soils are softer than virgin soil and offer poorer footing for troops, vehicles and field guns."[7]

No matter how porous or permeable, soil consists of mineral and organic matter. Mud's mineral component contains particles in a variety of sizes, the three most important being (from larger to smaller) sand, silt, and clay. Ranging in size from ¼ inch to 3 inches in diameter, gravel is too large to *form* soil, but it does *occur* in soil. Conversely, gravel is more often a material used to stabilize and counter the effects of mud.[8] Sand remains loose when dry and compacts when wet. Silt is smaller than sand, and dry silt raises dust clouds under windy conditions. However, saturated silt can become soft, slippery mud until warmth or wind solidifies it again by drying. The smallest major soil particle is clay, which does not dry quickly and heaves when exposed to freezing

Third Armored Division soldiers clean the mud from their tank's treads while waiting to go into action near Stolberg, Germany. *U.S. Army Military History Institute*

and thawing temperatures. All of these particles appear in pure forms, but combinations are more common, and they modify each basic soil type, depending on the mix.[9] In the Appendix, Table 1 clarifies soil moisture and particle size interaction.

Oddly, although most soils become less stable with increased moisture, sandy soil reacts differently. Sand particles allow moisture to percolate down from the surface more quickly, and the cohesion of any remaining moisture makes sandy soil firm underfoot.[10] Although combatants prefer wet sand to dry for marching purposes, when building airfields in the South Pacific, dry sand has served as a better base for matting.[11] As with all other soils, however, when supersaturated, even sand loses its stability. Pursuing the German Afrika Korps after the battle at El Alamein in Egypt in 1942, British forces encountered a series of severe storms inundating the desert, making for almost impossible conditions for trucks and tanks to continue.[12] A more unusual combination of sand and moisture occurred during the 2003 war in Iraq when a sandstorm halted offensive operations for American forces. The sandstorm created a situation alien to many Americans when heavy rains trapped large amounts of sand in the air. John Burns, correspondent for the *New York Times,* spoke of "mud rain,"[13] while Capt. Jason Conroy, author of *Heavy Metal,* noted, "Mud was actually falling from the sky. Rain was falling through the dust storm, picking up dirt, and falling as wet, gooey mud. It was starting to coat everything."[14]

In 1944, U.S. Army personnel conducted a series of tests, which defined mud's types in the process. To make the best use of the nation's limited rubber resources and to ensure that its soldiers accomplished their missions, the testers needed to know the most efficient use of low-pressure tires. Using 2½-ton and 4-ton trucks carrying specified loads, the Army held "mud traction, mud flotation, and 'go-no-go'" trials. As a result, mud was classified into two types and two subtypes. Setting the necessary parameters for mud, the report stated, "There is nothing constant about mud. It meant any one of an infinite number of variations of soil and water from a slippery slimy layer over a firm base to a bottomless quagmire resembling quicksand in its action." Any infantryman in any historical era would nod his head in knowing agreement.

Despite mud's enormous variations, the army experts did identify types of mud as Type I, which is "bottomless," and Type II, which includes all other types of mud not covered by Type I. "Bottomless" means that the mud's consistency cannot support a vehicle with tires set at 20 pounds of pressure or that mud has a hard layer that exists deeper than the vehicle's ground clearance. Type IIa mud has a cleaning quality (a high enough moisture content to work as liquid) while Type IIb is highly adhesive and lacks any cleaning quality.[15]

Before delving much further into mud's influence on military history, it is necessary to explain some of mud's characteristics and effects. Mud's main characteristics are its softness, adhesiveness, and lubricity. Mud's churnability, capacity to dampen explosions, and ability to create suction are its three effects. Mud's use as an obscurant is an application.

Softness is a quality found in all of mud's types. However, it is most associated with Type I mud because of its inability to support a vehicle.

Mud's softness has positive and negative effects on combatants. Many falls capable of producing serious injury or death have been less severe because mud softened the blow. After leading the famous raid on Tokyo, Gen. James (Jimmy) Doolittle parachuted into China as his bomber ran out of fuel. Forced to hit silk, Doolittle recalled that he landed without injury in a muddy rice paddy.[16] In the same way, U.S. Army medic Daniel (Doc) Evans survived a helicopter crash in Vietnam when he jumped from the craft before it struck ground. Leaping out of the stricken helicopter, Evans attempted to dive into a nearby river but overshot his intended landing zone. Luckily, he landed in a rice paddy in a few feet of water and a "foot or so of soft mud."[17]

Mud's softness allows heavier materials to compress it. Being run over by any large vehicle usually means death, but when the ground is soft mud, miracles can happen. For example, an American artilleryman fighting in Italy during World War II had soft mud to thank for saving his foot. As he attempted to hitch an artillery piece to a truck, the gun trail slipped and landed on his foot. Since he stood in soft mud, the gun pressed his foot down a few inches rather than shattering his bone. From that point forward, he "quit griping about the mud."[18] Sgt. Allen Towne, a U.S. Army medic, recalled another incident in which an American soldier appreciated mud's softness. When a truck ran over his legs as he slept, the infantryman's legs did not break, but sank into the soft ground, leaving him with only a few bruises.[19]

While in the army, the author received numerous warnings against sleeping under tanks when the ground was dry. Sudden rains could saturate the soil enough for tracked vehicles, weighing thousands of pounds, to sink slowly. Although the excessive weight of a tank might not crush a sleeping soldier, it could smother an individual underneath and attempting to drive the vehicle out could prove even more hazardous.

Additionally, tank tracks left in anything but Type I mud made travel easier for soldiers who could then walk in the mud ruts. Sgt. Karl Fuchs, a German tanker, wrote that whenever his unit took its vehicles through sodden fields, the tanks left deep furrows behind, which came in handy for foot soldiers.[20] German infantryman Gottlob Bidermann remembered plodding through the mud while marching in the Crimea. He preferred the tracks made by his gun mover to the prospect of stomping through the soft mud.[21] Likewise, tank tracks have provided an emergency entrenchment. Moving across an open field, one American infantryman in Hardt, Germany, took cover in a German tank track 6 inches deep. The soft mud provided at least some emergency cover even if it was not an ideal shelter from small arms fire.[22]

Ease of digging fortifications in mud also benefitted soldiers. U.S. Marine E. B. Sledge recalled that shoveling in Okinawa's soft mud was much easier than hacking at Peleliu's coral rock.[23] Soldiers made incredible progress clawing at the soil when their life depended on it, but digging in the mud was that much easier. Trying to avoid the shrapnel from a German 88mm gun, one group of American infantrymen lay flat on their stomachs and used their helmets to dig into the soft ground, creating hasty entrenchments a foot deep in minutes.[24]

Tanks and other vehicles driving through soft mud often leave signs of their presence. Having visible wheel or track marks can be detrimental to a mission. During World War I, the British forces desired to launch their new tanks with an element of surprise, which meant a careful approach. Tankers moved slowly and at night to reduce the chance of visual and audible detection. They also endeavored to drive over hard ground because soft mud left tracks visible to the air.[26]

Sticky mud appears most often in Type I and Type IIb mud, the latter being not so deep as to "exceed a vehicle's ground clearance" but "highly adhesive; with no cleaning quality."[25] Although not all mud is viscous, when its moisture content is low, it tends to be sticky. Consequently, Type IIa mud with its higher moisture

content and cleaning quality is not viscous.Sticky, cling-
ing mud adheres to combatant's footwear, adds more
weight, and increases levels of exhaustion and fatigue.
Lieutenant General Burns recalled that the Somme's
combination of saturated clay and chalk created an adhesive mud that stuck to his boots in large clods and
made walking laborious.[27] After receiving orders to move
his guns and ammunition from one location to another
along a route deep in sticky mud, one consternated British artillery officer remarked, "I am half expecting orders to bring along an acre of ground with me, too."[28]
Lt. Gordon Lee Mallonee, an American naval officer,
noted while ashore on Guadalcanal that nearby islands
had a coral base but that the fighting on Guadalcanal
had occurred in the mud. He wrote that he would "vouch
for the authenticity of any statements concerning mud
that is so thick it pulls high-top shoes off."[29]

The liquid nature of Type IIa mud makes it easy
to wipe away or remove, but thick adhesive mud is
more challenging, especially for mechanized soldiers.
Driving a truck in the Soviet Union, Guy Sajer recalled following a tank that had turned the saturated
soil into something resembling molasses. Eventually
his windshield "became completely caked with mud,"
and his assistant driver had to scrape the mud away
with his hand. Shortly thereafter, mud covered the narrow strip of the blackout light completely and Sajer could
only drive by leaning out of his window to try and "see
through the flying mud spun up by our wheels."[30] For
armored fighting vehicles moving under combat conditions, a member of the crew could not simply wipe clean
a mud-caked periscope. Advancing along the Scottish
corridor in late June 1944, Churchill tank driver Cyril
Rees recalled his dilemma when ordered to drive with
his hatch closed. As thick mud obscured his periscopes,
he had to decide whether to open his hatch to see, stop

the tank and clean the periscopes, or do nothing. He chose the latter and ended up stuck in an antitank ditch.[31]

The final characteristic of mud is lubricity. None of mud's types lay sole claim to mud's slickness, although Type I mud may not seem as slippery as Type II. The degree of lubricity depends on having at least some mud atop a hard surface on which to slide; hence bottomless mud is not as slippery for combatants.

If veterans cannot recall mud's depth or adhesiveness, they do remember slipping and sliding in it. Recounting one night in January 1918, stretcher bearer Frank Dunham wrote that the trenches were full of thigh-deep clay, miring soldiers where they stood. Wishing to avoid this obstacle, he and some others decided to move along the top, but merely crawling out of the slippery-sided trenches was an accomplishment. Unfortunately, the surface above the trenches was "like glass and chaps were slipping over in the dark every minute, so we slid back into the trench again."[32]

Vehicles, even all-wheel drive and fully tracked varieties, can slide in the mud. Despite the great weight of such machines and the intrinsic power available in their wheels and tracks, mud can prove resilient to their force. German officers describing river crossings in the Soviet Union remembered that mud "coated the roads with a slippery, soap-like surface." They added that when the conditions were right, mechanized vehicles slid down valleys, if they did not overturn, and were incapable of climbing the other side.[33] Riding in a tank across the Soviet Union was Karl Fuchs's usual mode of transportation, but in a letter to his wife, he explained the difficulties of simple movement during the Russian muddy season. "Even walking has become a feat. It is very difficult to stay on your feet—that's how slippery it is."[34] The U.S. Army's 133rd Infantry Regiment encountered one frightening aspect of mud's slippery quality. Failing to complete a mine-clearing operation in October 1944, the Second Battalion was scheduled to finish the job the next night. In the meantime, however, mud from a heavy rain caused the mines to *slip* from their previously marked positions.[35]

Of mud's three effects, its churnability is especially significant. Churning describes how outside forces—human, animal, vehicle, or explosive—can create more mud. Soil damp from rain or thaw is not necessarily mud. As long as a soil retains its original undisturbed state (a condition established over numerous years), it can resist the effects of these forces. However, when soil is disturbed, these initial formations collapse. Although particle size is a major determinant in the type of mud produced, agitation of saturated soil also shapes it. Churning is an effect that produces all types of mud. For example, if supersaturated soil is excessively stressed it can produce Type I mud. If moisture content is high, increased agitation suspends soil particles, creating Type IIa mud. Lower moisture content and constant action causes adhesion—Type IIb.

A GI working on a road in Italy in 1944 experiences

Before the Industrial Age, humans, horses, and nonmotorized wheels churned sodden ground into mud, but when the Industrial Age began, wheels that were once propelled by human or animal power received greater power. With more torque, motorized wheels dug into the surfaces until they encountered resistance, thus achieving motion. Further technological advances brought tracked vehicles, which had greater mobility over soft terrain but also an increased ability to tear the soil.

In fact, the passage of a single tank company could churn a meadow into soft mud and did it faster if the soil was under cultivation.[36] "Even gravel and some hard-surfaced roads" became quagmires if churned by heavy traffic.[37] Tracked vehicles caused such damage to Okinawa's roads that military police restricted the speed limit of tanks to "5 miles per hour and cautioned them against excessive tracking."[38] Lieutenant General Burns remembered that the Italian winter of 1944 seemed to repeat his miserable experiences in World War I. He reasoned that although the Italian campaign was not entirely a static one, the mud and mountainous terrain caused offensives to stall and distinct defensive lines to develop. Burns recounted how feet, wheels, and tracks churned saturated soil into "the soldier's ancient enemy—mud,"[39] which had a direct effect on military potential.[40] For example, at the Battle of Waterloo, one British regiment churned the ground into knee-deep mud when it repeatedly changed from square to column on the same spot.[41] Knowing something about operations in exceptionally muddy conditions, German general Dr. Lothar Rendulic explained, "Roads used during the mud periods are soon churned up to such a depth that further traffic becomes more and more difficult until it stops altogether."[42]

Churned mud progressively slows movement. As the first few soldiers or vehicles move along a pristine route, the effects of their movement increase the difficulty for those who follow. Tokugawa Ieyasu's cavalry and foot soldiers churned the approach road to Sekigahara in 1600 so severely it significantly slowed his follow-on forces.[43] Following other units along muddy roads caused British infantry officer Siegfried Sassoon's unit to take 3-1/2 hours to move a little more than a mile.[44] In October 1941, the Seventh Panzer Division recorded that only a few hours of continued traffic turned the roads bottomless and follow-on units could not maintain the march rates set by the first units.[45] Likewise, the six march groups of the German Twenty-fourth Panzer Division tried to move between sectors of World War II's Eastern Front. The first group covered 47 miles in 15 hours but the next group barely made 6 miles. Although the normally dirt roads used were muddy before the first march group crossed them, they became progressively worse. The poor performance of the second march unit derived from this heavy use.[46]

Churned mud hinders mobile formations from using their advantage in speed and maneuverability. Typically, cavalry has both assets in its favor, but mud's churnability often equalizes the clash between cavalry and infantry. For example, mud hampered horse and rider sufficiently in February 1593 for samurai to overpower Chinese horsemen. The cavalry had churned the battlefield, already soaked by snowmelt, into a morass of mud.[47] In addition, Napoleon's Old Guard at Waterloo struggled toward the British through mud that French cavalry exacerbated with its numerous failed charges.[48]

High explosives also churn saturated soil into mud. Concerning tactics on World War I's Western Front, Lieutenant General Burns emphasized that high explosives tore the ground so effectively as to cause their attacks to fail.[49] In June 1944, Otto Carius, a German tank officer, noted that an offensive against Soviet troops proved difficult because artillery fire from friend and foe ripped the ground into a muddy morass.[50]

Relating closely to mud's softness is its capacity to dampen explosive impacts. Type I and Type IIb muds have the greatest dampening effect on explosions, while Type IIa's high moisture content does not dampen a weapon's impact like the other types but sometimes splashes mud without reducing the destructive force of the explosion.

Artillery shells do detonate in mud (though not always), but they often lose much of their effectiveness as mud dampens the concussive effect of the explosion and shrapnel's dispersal. During the American Civil War, Gen. Alpheus Williams had an artillery shell strike directly beneath his horse, "throwing up the mud like a volcano." He found, to his surprise, that his horse had three or four wounds but none were serious. Williams surmised that the shell buried itself deep in the soft mud until it struck harder material, concluding, "The superincumbent pressure gave a low direction to the pieces, and thus saved both horse and myself."[51] While fighting in the Carpathian Mountains, 1st Lt. Erwin Rommel noticed a correlation among a high percentage of duds, the ineffectiveness of shrapnel, and soft mud.[52] During the Vietnam War Gy.Sgt. Allan Jay Kellogg Jr. reacted to an enemy hand grenade by pushing the bomb into the mud and throwing himself on top of it. Although the explosion should have killed him, mud diminished the grenade's force.[53] Its dampening ability did not save Pvt. Anthony L. Krotiak, who used the mud around him to save fellow soldiers, an action for which he received a posthumous Medal of Honor. Fighting the Japanese on Luzon, Krotiak reacted immediately to an enemy grenade that landed among his squad. Using his rifle butt, he jammed the grenade into the soft mud and then fell on top of it, saving his men but losing his life.[54]

Suction is another of mud's effect. Type IIb's adhesiveness holds combatants and material with suction. The deeper the mud (the closer it is to Type I mud) the greater the suctioning effect, but Type IIa's high moisture content has the least capacity to hold combatants or their material.

As mud loses some of its moisture and becomes more adhesive, it develops a suctioning effect, which plagues combatants. Maj. Paul Grauwin, the senior French medical officer, remembered how the mud at Dien Bien Phu turned to putty after a two-day absence of rain, and if he wished to walk in this "glue," he had to make every effort to pull his boots from it. The suctioning effect became worse when he operated, at which time he often stood in one place for an hour while the mud encased him and forced him to wrench his feet from it.[55]

Losing footwear to suction is another mud-induced annoyance some combatants have experienced. At Waterloo the mud caused some French soldiers to lose their boots, marching in formation hampered their ability to retrieve them.[56] An American veteran of the Italian campaign remembered for the television series *The World at War*, "If anybody was in the galoshes business he could have found them by the millions along the roadside, because you couldn't walk with them. I mean it was impossible to go through that mud."[57] General Rendulic recollected that deep mud in the Soviet Union during World War II even pulled the shoes from horses' hooves.[58]

Knowing that sucking mud would steal their footwear, some veterans removed their boots. During the Peloponnesian War, combatants wore a shoe on their left foot only to prevent themselves from "slipping in the mud,"[59] and Medal of Honor recipient Sgt. John Basilone, realizing that Guadalcanal's mud would pull at his feet and inhibit his freedom of action, removed his boots rather than lose them in the mud.[60]

As combatants have sunk to greater depths in Type I mud, its suction has prevented them from breaking free. When mud is lower than a person's thigh, his or her chances of breaking mud's seal are feasible without assistance, but for combatants stuck in mud above the knee, the prospect of recovery unaided diminishes. In January 1918, Frank Dunham witnessed how. "Some [soldiers] even had to leave their waders stuck in the mud, and wriggle their legs free, to finish the journey in stockinged feet."[61]

Freeing an individual unaided from mud's suction is difficult, and for vehicles assistance is often necessary. Tanks in World War II required two American T-2 recovery vehicles, each with a 50-ton winch, to be freed. Lt. Belton Cooper, an American army officer, noted that when tanks became mired deep enough to obscure most of their track they began to act "like huge suction cups" and recovery teams had "to dig small slit trenches under the back and sides of the tanks to let air underneath and break the vacuum."[62] In a similar way, Rexile Hamric operated a tank retriever in Vietnam and recalled that mud's suctioning effect could be so powerful that engineers sometimes used small amounts of C-4 explosive to remove immobilizing mud.[63]

Mud's suctioning effect also could hinder helicopters. Serving as a Huey door gunner in Vietnam, Spc. 4 Matt Jones recalled one incident when mud nearly captured his helicopter. Jones explained that after setting down in a muddy location, "with the top of the skids barely visible," when the pilot tried to lift off, "the mud grabbed us." As the pilot struggled with the helicopter, Jones remembered hearing a sucking sound and feeling the aircraft shake from the power required to break free.[64]

Less an effect and more of an application, mud can obscure (often purposefully as camouflage) combatants and their equipment. Type I is especially conducive to hiding materials. Type IIb works well as a camouflage as it adheres when applied while Type IIa is least efficient because its high moisture content permits mud to "clean" away.

Mud's use as camouflage is an excellent example of this application. American soldiers fighting in the Pacific Theater found that using "generous applications of mud concealed white faces from enemy eyes."[65] However, using mud as camouflage for the face is more often a field expedient. Knowing that mud contains numerous bacteria that can infect open wounds, most combatants seeking facial camouflage use burnt cork, the ash from an automobile exhaust, or manufactured camouflage paints.

Although combatants sometimes use mud to camouflage their faces, they are even more likely to use it to remove the shine or markings from equipment. The U.S. Army's Quartermaster Museum notes that one of the motivations for converting from blue uniforms to khaki came during the Spanish-American War. "The blue coats of U.S. troops fighting in Cuba presented such visible targets to snipers that the men smeared mud on their uniforms to be less conspicuous."[66] With their preference for edged weapons and use of night infiltration tactics, many Japanese patrols camouflaged the gleam of their bayonets with mud. Capt. Suzuki Tadashi remembered a battalion night attack when his soldiers dulled their bayonets with mud as did L. Cpl. Sakano Toshiyuki, who recalled that his unit had fixed bayonets and pasted them with mud "so that they did not reflect light."[67] As modern armies use nets and patterns of paint to help obscure their equipment, military units have and will continue to use mud as camouflage. Matt Jones found little logic in having large white markings looking like targets on the underside of his helicopter. To rectify this incongruity, the pilot of Jones's helicopter deliberately hovered low above any large mud puddle or rice paddy using the mud brought up from the rotor wash to obscure the white markings.[68]

Combatants use mud, especially Type I, as a concealment source. At Dien Bien Phu, Grauwin received word from his stretcher bearers that the Viet Minh, appeared suddenly in large numbers, rising from the mud that hid them.[69] Although mud is often deliberately chosen as a concealment agent, being muddy because of combat can also prove beneficial. Fighting at close quarters in the Crimea, Henry Metelmann, a German tank driver, dove into a mudhole to hide from approaching Soviet troops. Luckily for him, his muddy covering and inactivity hid him from their advance. As the Soviets sought subsequent concealment from a German counterattack, they joined Metelmann, still unaware of his presence, in the mudhole. Since the German soldiers returning fire "could not distinguish between the mud-

Looking like an amphibious plane, a B-24 taxies down the muddy runway of its base in Italy during World War II.
U.S. Army Military History Institute

clad figures as German or Russian, they could not make use of their machine guns."[70] More recently, Taliban forces, during the 2003 American intervention in Afghanistan used mud to conceal their vehicles from American aircraft.

Type I mud more so than Type II can hide dangers within it. Because the mud in his hospital bunker was so excessive, Grauwin recalled a desire to work in his bare feet "but concealed in the mud there were broken needles and glass which cut the soles of the feet."[71] Another danger obscured by mud was unexploded munitions, which often had failed to detonate in the soft soil. A British trench limerick of World War I adequately portrayed this hazard.

> There was a young man of Avesnes,
> Took a stroll down a long shady lesnes,
> He trod on a dud
> Half hidden in mud. . . !
> He never will do it agesnes.[72]

Mud appears on the battlefield in three ways, each of which is the subject of a subsequent chapter. First, some mud, found in swamps for instance, exists on a permanent basis. Second, mud appears in geographical areas that have predictable periods of excessive precipitation and consequently large amounts of mud. The mud produced in monsoons and muddy seasons such as the Russian *rasputiza* are examples of seasonal mud. Last, the unpredictable appearances of mud from heavy rainfall or sudden thaw are examples of random mud.

CHAPTER 2

Permanent Mud

"Those who do not know the conditions of mountains and forests, hazardous defiles, marshes and swamps, cannot conduct the march of an army."[1]

—*Sun-tzu*

Mud influences military operations from the single combatant to entire armies and its ability to degrade—if not completely halt—an offensive is its greatest influence. Commanders know that mud hinders troop movements and most avoid large areas of mud if they know of its presence.

Permanent mud occurs most frequently in wetlands—geographic features such as swamps, marshes, and sloughs. Wetlands are either seasonal or perennial, but unless the dry season is severe, the inherent soggy nature of a wetland warns the wary that mud is a predictable terrain component. Therefore, mud is permanent in areas identified on a map as a wetland no matter the season.[2] Combatants have difficulty defining mud and just as many cannot properly identify geographic features. For example, a swamp is "a general term applied to a permanently waterlogged area and its associated veg-

etation, commonly reeds." Slough is a very accurate term
for "a piece of soft, miry, or muddy ground . . . impassable to heavy vehicles," though few writers ever refer to
such terrain as a slough. The major difference between
a marsh and a swamp is that a marsh might not always
contain water while a swamp is always saturated.[3] Type
I and Type II mud exists in wetlands and swamps, but
these geographic features are more likely to contain Type
I mud than the unpredictable mud produced by a thunderstorm. Joseph Markey, writing a history of Iowa Volunteers in the Spanish-American War, made this state-
ment about a Philippine swamp: "A swamp is repulsive
to even think of, and more so to move in. This one was a
muck of foul mud and mixed with decayed vegetation."[4]

Wetlands exist all over the globe (except on Antarc-
tica). Finding permanent mud in a desert may seem odd
to many people, but it affected the Battle of El Alamein.
The Qattara Depression, "a sudden sea of quicksand and
salt marsh impassable to tanks,"[5] was not like any other
portion of desert fought over in World War II. It prevented the Axis forces from exploiting their enemy's
flanks as they had in earlier battles. The Qattara
Depression's permanent mud forced the Axis to fight in
a confined area.

Knowing of mud's existence or accurately predicting its arrival benefits commanders. Mud is an ally of
the defender and competent commanders use mud to
their advantage. The U.S. Army developed the abbreviation, OCOKA (Observation, Cover, Obstacles, Key
Terrain, Avenues of Approach) to aid leaders in finding
the best defensive positions.[6] The U.S. Marine Corps
uses a similar abbreviation—KOCOA, the key words
remain but the order of precedence differs.

Mud makes an excellent obstacle. Placing entrenchments behind wetlands or large areas of Type I mud capable of miring the enemy not only slows or stops ar-

mored vehicles, it also hinders (if not halts) cavalry and infantry. Commanders also use mud to affect any avenues of approach the enemy might use. On hard surface roads (provided they have little or no damage from battle or deliberate cratering attempts) mud has little influence. However, off-road approach routes are a different matter. Knowing how mud hinders cross-country movement is one way for commanders to identify defensible terrain.[7]

Some commanders have had the forethought to incorporate mud into their defensive schemes. Ancient and medieval battles frequently took place when a defender chose a piece of terrain to defend, and battles only occurred when the attacker felt confident of victory. Scottish commanders habitually used marshes against the English armies of King Edward I and his son King Edward II. The famed Scottish commander William Wallace defeated one English army by using

A Ninth Infantry soldier makes his way through Mekong River mud near Rash Kien, Vietnam, in 1967. *U.S. Army Military History Institute*

the tactical defensive and placing his men behind a swamp. Following his example, Robert the Bruce also took up defensive positions with wetlands either to his front or flanks. On two occasions, he forced the English to either go around the mud or move slowly through it. As shock and speed were the strengths of English heavy cavalry, slowly navigating a way through marshy terrain denied them their greatest asset.[8]

The permanent mud of wetlands has also affected battles since the Industrial Revolution. During Napoleon Bonaparte's Polish campaign of 1806, Russian infantry stood in bogs waist deep, where they were safe from attack by cavalry.[9] Looking back at the Battle of Passchendaele, even Field Marshal Sir Douglas Haig conceded his strategic goal of the Belgian coast after four days of constant rain, which had turned "the shell-torn valleys into almost impassable bogs." Two of his generals, Sir Herbert Plumer and Sir Hubert Gough, wanted to halt the offensive earlier because of the oppressive mud, but Haig insisted on gaining the high ground near Passchendaele. Canadian infantry officer E. L. M. Burns remembered that continuing assaults in poor conditions would not lead to defeat of the Germans because "mud is the ally of the defenders and the enemy of the attackers."

The fighting at Passchendaele was so difficult because the area was originally a swamp and the fighting had destroyed the elaborate ditching and drainage systems. Subsequently, "the land reverted to the primeval bog, except that all trees, bushes, and other vegetation had disappeared under the storm of high explosives, and there remained only mud."[10] While fighting near the Narwa bridgehead in late March 1944, German tank commander Otto Carius recalled that "operations in marshes are unpleasant and, at the same time, unsatisfying for any tanker."[11]

The Battle of New Orleans may not have turned on the presence of permanent mud, but the use of a cypress swamp to anchor Gen. Andrew Jackson's line in 1815 was essential. The surprise appearance of British troops under Gen. Edward Pakenham within eight miles of New Orleans forced Jackson to choose a battlefield.

General Pakenham's intention was to march up the city side (eastern bank of the Mississippi River at that point) toward his prize—New Orleans. Both sides of the river had plantations that reached a few hundred meters at most from the river to cypress swamps. In addition, the American forts located on the river denied the British a free route and American ships controlled the river above the forts. Although it was possible, it would have been dangerous for Pakenham to attempt crossing his force to the west side of the river and then back across to the city side until the American ships were neutralized. Although Jackson had Gen. David B. Morgan build a line on the western side of the river, he correctly determined that the British approach would be on the city side.

General Jackson's main line of defense was a rampart built along the Rodriguez Canal. He chose this location because it was the shortest line from the river to the "thick and almost impenetrable swamp."[12] The canal was a dry, grass-covered ditch approximately 11 feet wide and at least 4 feet deep.[13] Jackson quickly realized that digging was not an option for his line. The ground, being so close to the river and a swamp, was too wet to allow digging to any depth. For the protection of his soldiers and guns, he would have to erect a wall of mud. Author Robert Remini noted in *The Battle of New Orleans* that although Jackson chose to use the river and swamp to secure his flanks, he initially failed to extend his line *into* the swamp leaving "a good bit of dry land undefended"; however, local sailor and pirate Jean Lafitte brought the matter to Jackson's attention, and the general promptly extended his line to the swamp.[14]

The Americans made unique use of mud as they built their defensive line. Here was one of the rare uses of liquid-heavy mud, as opposed to adobe or mud bricks, in the construction of a defensive work. Jackson's men built a rampart and placed guns along it. Mud's plasticity does not make it the best material for building, but it was all that was available to the Americans. To correct the instability of mud, they took cypress logs and built cribs and brought in firmer soil from other areas to try and stiffen the mud. Eventually, they built their wall 3 to 4 feet from the ground, but including the ditch before it, the distance from the bottom of the canal to the top of the rampart was closer to 7 or 8 feet.[15]

The canal gave Jackson a head start as his soldiers built the rampart behind it, but the key to his position was its secure flanks. Control of the Mississippi River secured one end of his line while the swamp secured the other. The British assault would come directly at Jackson's line as they realized the difficulty of turning these flanks. Lt. Col. Alexander Dickson, the British artillery commander, described the terrain leading to Jackson's line as a dense growth of cypress trees and muddy ground that made the approach "in every respect impracticable." If Dickson's word were not enough, Lt. Peter Wright of the Engineers reported to Pakenham that "the cypress swamp would foil any attempt to turn the flank opposed to the British right."[16]

The use of artillery was one challenging aspect of fighting in a swamp. Before the main assault began, the British launched an artillery assault on the American position. One of the first problems the British encountered was their inability to properly protect the guns and their crews, for to move into position to fire on the American position meant they were susceptible to returned fire.

One of the materials Lieutenant Colonel Dickson found was sugar barrels, which he had filled with mud. Dickson discovered quickly that he could not dig into the swampy terrain, so he constructed firing positions above ground with whatever materials he could acquire. On the American side, Jackson had placed his guns "on wooden platforms that rested on cotton bales laid three deep to prevent them from sinking into the mud."[17]

Mud influenced the outcome of the artillery duel. Some of the British guns, without proper flooring in their firing positions, fired only two or three rounds, "driving themselves into the mud and out of action." Conversely, the mud worked to the benefit of the Americans. The British bombardment had damaged some of Jackson's guns and destroyed some ammunition, but it did not harm the rampart in any noticeable way as British "cannonballs simply buried themselves in the thick mud walls without puncturing them or causing them to collapse."

Even after the artillery duel was over, the British were hampered further by the necessity of retrieving their guns from the mud. Pakenham's soldiers knew from moving the guns into position that dragging ship's guns, still in their naval carriages, was exhausting. Under cover of darkness they dug the heavy cannons from deep mud and then dragged them back to British lines. They finished the job at four in the morning.[18]

Since the British could not circumvent the river and still remain on the eastern bank, the only end of Jackson's line they could realistically outflank was through the swamp. In late December 1814, the British sent a small number of soldiers through the swamp to attempt turning Jackson's line. They failed, and the swamps played a role in their failure. Robert Remini noted that Jackson had positioned frontiersmen from Tennessee in the swamp. These men knew how to live and fight in such terrain. They moved gracefully through the swamp "leaping like cats from log to log" and thought nothing of wading through the mud. On the other hand, the British feared the swamp.[19]

When the assault finally arrived on January 8, 1815, Jackson's position connecting a swamp with a mud rampart once again frustrated British efforts. The placement of the American line forced the British to cross 2,000 yards of open, muddy ground. In addition, the mud rampart was 14 to 20 feet thick and had already proven impervious to artillery. Because of poor leadership or miscommunication, the British assaulted the mud rampart without the scaling ladders needed to breach the fortification in place. Hence, members of the Rifle Brigade advance guard rushed into the ditch before the mud wall and attempted "to cut their way up the rampart with their bayonets."[20] As more British soldiers arrived they attempted "to scale the parapet, but without ladders they could not reach the top. They scrambled up the wall as best they could and got just so far before sliding down into the soft mud."[21]

Mud influences the performance of tanks. The track system, designed for use in fields, that differentiates a tank from a truck is vulnerable to mud, especially Type I. Tanks generally have good cross-country mobility but their success in mud depends greatly on their weight and track width. To operate well in mud, a tank needs to spread its weight over the soft ground. According to Belton Cooper, "the key to a tank's off-road mobility is its ground-bearing pressure: how the weight of the tank is distributed over the ground,"[22] which derives from its total weight compared to its track width.[23]

An excellent example of ground-bearing pressure's significance for tracked vehicles was the U.S. Army's M4 Sherman tank. This World War II-era vehicle had a poor ground pressure of 7 pounds per square inch.

Although this number was similar to what an infantry-man exerted, it was twice the pressure of German tanks. When late-model Shermans arrived with 3 to 4 tons of additional armor, yet the same narrow tracks, the tank's mobility degraded further. For the Americans, the M26 Pershing tank was better in muddy conditions. The Pershing, despite weighing 13 tons more than the Sherman, had "a ground bearing pressure of three square inches" versus the Sherman's seven, making it "comparable to the German tanks in negotiating soft, muddy terrain."[24]

Track width did not save exceedingly heavy tanks and self-propelled guns from the mud. German soldiers knew that despite the Ferdinand assault gun's heavy punch, its weight was too much for Russian mud. Günter Koschorrek, a German infantryman, observed that despite having extra-wide tracks to support its 75 tons, mud was one of the gun's "worst enemies capable of rendering them totally immobile" and added that Russian mud did not allow the Ferdinand to be placed in the best tactical positions.[25]

One modification that improved a tank's ground bearing pressure was the addition of track extenders. The U.S. Army recognized the Sherman's poor performance in mud and created a modification kit to correct the deficiency by adding "3-inch-wide steel grousers, attached to the track connectors on each track block." These track extenders increased the width of the tank's track to 20 inches, and thus spread more of its weight over the soft ground and increased its performance (but still less than the 30 to 36 inches on German tank tracks). Cooper noted that the grousers were helpful, but American tanks "still got stuck easily."[26]

Flail tanks had their own problems with mud, the depth of Type I and the adhesiveness of Type IIb mud proving especially burdensome. To detonate mines, a flail tank used chains attached to rotating drums several feet in front of its hull. In November 1944, American flail tanks attacked German positions, but muddy fields resisted the power applied to the flail's drum robbing the tracks of the necessary force to advance. Subsequently, when the flail tanks failed to detonate mines as the attack began they became stuck in the mud instead.[27] During the 1945 British Reichswald offensive, flail tanks found that despite the danger of mines "it was the mud which proved the greater deterrent. Within half an hour three tracks had become so badly bogged they were quite useless."[28]

Some examples of mud's metaphors merit inclusion here. Historically, numerous terms and descriptions of mud offer further evidence that mud is not constant. In a letter to a Knox College student, Lt. John Campbell wrote his own opinions of mud:

Soldiers of the U.S. Third Brigade, Ninth Infantry Division, team up to deal with the mud of the upper Mekong delta. *U.S. Army Military History Institute*

Georgia has the red clay kind, slippery going uphill. (I've never met anyone going in any other direction in Georgia.) Florida's mud is wet and sandy, packs wet and is good for cleaning mess kits. England has soupy mud that doesn't play square. If you're on a brick walk, at some point where bricks come together you'll cause a geyser of brown mud to shoot up and spatter your clothes. French and Belgian muds vary from thin paste to huge chunks. They peel easily in strips like dough for pie crust before it's been baked.[29]

Written accounts of mud and warfare describe mud in a variety of ways. Many veterans have used different metaphors in attempts to describe a substance that is difficult to define, but food, something to which everyone related, is one of the more interesting.

One common edible description for mud is as porridge, only thicker. Lumpier muds such as Type I or Type IIb warrant that comparison. Maj. Gen. Sir Wilmot Herringham, a British medical officer, described a thaw-induced mud on the Western Front as "a kind of porridge,"[30] and after receiving orders to strengthen his position at Passchendaele, one British soldier retorted, "it is impossible to consolidate porridge."[31] In Burma, Gen. William Slim, commander of the British Fourteenth Army, wrote how his soldiers struggled "across steep slopes through mud with the consistency of porridge."

Mud has also been compared to chocolate. In early October 1944, General Slim referred to a 7-mile stretch of the Tiddim road: "No soldier who marched up the Chocolate Staircase is ever likely to forget the name or the place." While positioning an M48 tank, Lt. Lamar Myers, commander of an American engineer company in Vietnam, described the mud beneath an abandoned rice paddy: "It wasn't soft, and it wasn't hard. It was like the consistency of a warmed chocolate syrup, not hot chocolate syrup. It wasn't cold, so it was stiff, but warm."[32]

Myers, deciding that his description of mud was not accurate enough for his conscience, elaborated on his earlier depiction and compared it to two other edibles, stating that the mud "was thick, but it was gooey—molasses thick, thick honey, something like that."[33] Explaining to his readers just how slick the red mud was along hillsides, Scott Gilmore, an American officer serving with Gurkhas in World War II, called it "greasy,"[34] and Lieutenant Campbell compared mud to a pie's "unbaked dough-like strips."[35] On March 24, 1945, an observation in a regimental journal from the First Armored Division reported that Schu mines brought back by a patrol were "caked in mud," and British soldiers at Passchendaele found it difficult to engage the enemy as their "rifles became so caked with mud that firing was impossible."[36]

In addition to food metaphors, those who experience a lot of mud in one area sometimes give names to their muddy location. In the American Civil War, Gen. Alpheus S. Williams wrote that his command journeyed 15 miles along the "Mudpike,"[37] and during the American intervention in Kosovo, soldiers from the Eighty-second Airborne Division named their growing base in Albania, "Mud World."[38] In 1863, Confederate forces near Tulahoma, Tennessee, explained, "that Tulahoma came from the Greek word 'tula' meaning mud and 'homa' meaning more mud."[39] Nearly a hundred years later the same pun reappeared but with different place names. While advancing toward Hoengsong, Korea, an anonymous marine claimed "that the word Hoengsong was from the ancient Greek 'Hoeng,' meaning mud, and 'Song,' meaning more mud."[40]

CHAPTER 3

Seasonal Mud

"The Blitzkrieg bogged down in mud."[1]
Department of the Army

"Three hundred miles and, with luck, some thirty days before the monsoon to do it in. It would be a close thing."[2] So wrote General Slim in his World War II memoir, *Defeat into Victory*. He fought successfully in Burma for many reasons, but one of them was his recognition of seasonal mud—a byproduct of the monsoon's power.

Seasonal mud is predictable. Commanders knowledgeable of a region's climate know when rains and subsequent mud will arrive. In specific regions and during particular months, climatic conditions and terrain factors bring seasonal mud. Examples of the climatic conditions that cause seasonal mud are the Russian mud season and Southeast Asian monsoons, while other regions also have predictable periods of rain, thaw, and mud.

The German invasion of the Soviet Union in June 1941 was one of the best examples of a military decision made without considering seasonal mud. Although they made great gains in the first four months, the Germans did not plan for Russia's mud season, an event that should not have caught them unaware. In fact, the mud season was such a part of Russian life that it had its own name—*rasputiza* (time without roads)—and occurred twice a year.[3] The first mud season came in the fall just before the onset of winter and the second arrived in the spring when the snow melted. What made the *rasputiza* different from mud that developed at any other time of the year was the greater frequency of Type I mud (although all types of mud existed). European Russia developed mud after summer storms, but conditions at that time of year precluded the creation of large predictable amounts of Type I mud. Increased clouds, cooler winds, and an increase in low-pressure storms enhanced the creation and duration of mud.

The *rasputiza* was a significant reason why the Germans failed to reach Moscow in 1941. Historians generally agree that the tardiness of Germany's invasion of the Soviet Union was one of several reasons for their failure to capture the Soviet capital. The Battle of Stalingrad may have turned the course of World War II in Europe, but Germany's opportunity to defeat the Soviet Union fell off sharply five months after Operation Barbarossa commenced, when they failed to take Moscow.[4] Germany's strategic planners had not foreseen and therefore were not ready for periods of limited mobility— a fault of German military intelligence. Hence, when the *rasputiza* arrived in 1941 "the Army was faced with a great calamity."[5]

The *rasputiza* was so effective because of German reliance on good roads and the Soviet Union's lack of them. In central and western Europe, macadamized roads were common, but "the only road in the Soviet Union paved to anything resembling Western standards was the one from Moscow through Smolensk to the old frontier."[6] Elsewhere in the Soviet Union, the Germans found that only 7 percent of roads were hard surface and the main roads in the eastern Soviet Union were gravel or dirt, which occasionally exhibited some signs of maintenance.[7] However, even roads with solid beds failed during the *rasputiza* if used too heavily and not maintained regularly. As the campaign continued and the dirt roads degraded, the Germans developed *rollbahns*: "traffic moving parallel to the original route but often yards away from it."[8] The Germans did try driving through the fields that bordered destroyed roads, but "a track once used could not be used again by another vehicle because it then became too deep," another example of mud's churnability.[9]

Gen. Heinz Guderian developed some idea of the *rasputiza's* significance when his initial encounters with summer rain showers "transformed the dirt roads into bottomless canals of mud." He knew his area of operations had no paved roads, and by late September, he made it an objective to secure "the good roads around Orel" before the *rasputiza* began. In doing so, he intended to create one reliable road as a supply route.[10] Even frontline soldiers perceived the *rasputiza's* power in summer showers. "When I see even at this time of year how our vehicles, after it's rained a little, can barely make the grade, I just can't imagine how it will be in autumn when the rainy period really sets in," wrote Wilhelm Prüller in his diary.[11]

Russian mud was what brought the vaunted blitzkrieg to a halt. The rains that created the *rasputiza* began in October's third week and lasted into the first week of November, and within days, the offensive slowed to a crawl, averaging 2 miles a day.[12] Some senior German officers observed that the *rasputiza's* appearance during the drive to Moscow seemed as if "nature suddenly put a protective wall around the Russian capital. It swallowed the most valuable equipment."[13] The *rasputiza* stopped the blitzkrieg because the German offensive system required dependable roads and good skies for flying.[14] In fact, German contempt for the muddy season surprised the Soviets who "did not expect the Germans to mount another all-out drive so close to the coming of the autumn rains."[15] Wheeled and tracked vehicles moved with great difficulty, if at all. Many German generals considered digging in until the spring as their tanks and trucks stopped in the mud.[16] They knew that as winter approached and the "Second Panzer Group lost 60 percent of its tanks to mud," it was best to halt and hold their gains.

Adolf Hitler was not fully aware of the *rasputiza's* effect and refused to stop his armies despite the recommendations of some senior generals to halt.[17] Instead, being so close to his objective of Moscow, he ordered the seizure of advanced bridgeheads, but the required roads needed for the advance disintegrated and German units halted. The German Seventh Panzer Division took "2 weeks to make a single routine move at an average speed of 3 or 4 kilometers per hour and with significant losses of vehicles and other material."[18] General Guderian understood that with vehicles "occasionally achieving a maximum speed of 12 miles per hour, there were no fast-moving units anymore"; and, concerning the führer's order to advance, he wrote in *Panzer Leader* that "Hitler was living in a world of fantasy."[19]

Not only were German combat units unable to advance toward Moscow, but resupply efforts slowed. The *rasputiza* halted the essential delivery of fuel and ammunition needed to continue. The 3-week halt in the advance doomed the German offensive as the severe Russian winter followed just weeks behind the *rasputiza*, and German troops found themselves in the open without winter fuel and winter clothing.[20]

The German blitzkrieg was derailed by mud, not the Russian winter. In fact, freezing temperatures allowed the vehicle advance to continue. The Germans, to their credit and in anticipation of continuing the offensive, actually anticipated the arrival of a frost heavy enough to harden the mud. Finally accepting the reality of the *rasputiza,* Adolf Hitler ordered his generals to advance "as soon as the ground hardened,"[21]and Guderian and Leo Geyr von Schweppenberg, one of his corps commanders, were already aware that they could continue the offensive once the frosts arrived.[22] Their drive on Moscow was able to continue on November 15, 1941.

European Russia receives great quantities of snow, and the subsequent spring thaw is predictable. The spring *rasputiza* occurs when large areas receive several days of above-freezing temperatures. (The random nature of smaller scale thaws, comprising a day or two of temperatures above freezing, appears in chapter 4.) The spring *rasputiza* was often worse than the fall version because spring rains combined with large amounts of snowmelt. Beginning around March 21, "terrible weather on the Eastern Front, wavering between freezing and thawing, heavy snow and rain, turned the Ukraine into a glutinous sea of mud."[23] Describing the affect of the spring muddy season on the steppes, German officers observed that the thaw dramatically altered the Soviet grasslands with the formation of many small ponds and larger, low-lying regions inundated with water. Gen. Dr. Lothar Rendulic believed that the spring *rasputiza* was worse than the fall because during winter the ground froze more than a meter deep. "As the surface gradually thaws downward, the ground which was cracked by the frost becomes first spongy and then mud. This process goes much deeper than would be the case because of rain alone."[24] German infantryman Gottlob Bidermann, serving in the Soviet Union's Courland region, found that "mid-March brought a thaw, reducing the streets and roads to little more than bottomless quagmires over which nothing could travel without great exertion." He noted that the spring *rasputiza* not only hindered the Germans, but "activity on the Soviet side came almost to a halt, the impassable roads spoiling any immediate plans for a further attack."[25]

Although the Germans had not prepared for the mud season on their initial entry into the Soviet Union, by the time the war had swung against them in 1943, they began to look on the *rasputiza* as an ally. The Soviets understood the *rasputiza*, but their lack of offensive experience in combination with the spring mud season hampered their own unit movements, and the construction of roads and forward airfields.[26] However, by 1944, the Soviets knew how to attack and plod through the spring mud. They intended to expel the Germans and advance into the Balkans, but the Germans believed that the *rasputiza* would stall the Soviets as it had hindered them.[27] Unfortunately for the Germans, the Soviets struggled through the spring thaw, when mud normally halted operations. The Germans never fully understood the *rasputiza* like the Soviets did.

The Soviets successfully advanced during 1944's spring *rasputiza* because they increased their level of motorization with large numbers of American-made four-wheel-drive trucks while the Germans relied on horse carts. Also, Soviet knowledge of their own country's climate was responsible for an important design element in the vaunted T34 tank. Admittedly, one reason for the greater cross-country performance of this tank versus its German opponent was the T34's wider tracks, which gave it a lower ground pressure. Although this was of great importance, Soviet tank designers in the 1930s, working with naval engineers, decided that maneuverability during the *rasputiza* would be more efficient if the tank's center of gravity was in the center. In March 1945 near Hungary, German mountain trooper Hans Jennewein observed the special mobility of these tanks when he remarked in an interview that mud slowed everything except T34s.[28] Heavy German tanks such as the Tiger and Panther had their center of gravity toward their front, which tended to cause them to nose into the mud and stay there—a situation all tank commanders would happily avoid.[29]

Instances abound concerning large numbers of vehicles that faltered in the Russian mud. An excellent example was the situation the Twenty-fourth Panzer (Armored) Division faced during 1944's spring *rasputiza*. Gen. Frido von Senger und Etterlin explained how serious the consequences were when higher commands did not understand the limitations of their equipment and disregarded the terrain and weather. One problem was the tremendous amount of fuel fully tracked vehicles used over short distances to free themselves and other vehicles. The supply trucks that supported the division were farther back in the march order and stuck. To alleviate this predicament, the division used horse-drawn carts as best they could, but the small loads carried by the carts were not enough to maintain the fuel supply the tanks demanded.[30]

General von Senger und Etterlin, because of his division's encounter with the *rasputiza*, listed some of the lessons learned, most of which involved the capability of different vehicle types. Although German staff cars were of little utility in the mud, they were light enough that soldiers could at least push them out when stuck in the mud. However, captured American-built jeeps only dug themselves in deeper and were much more difficult to dislodge. The Germans found their eight-wheeled armored cars to be mud mobile, but half-tracks and trucks with dual rear wheels sometimes caused Type IIb mud to clog their rollers and tires. One failing of German

vehicles when compared to those of American manu-
facture was that German vehicles always had a lower
power- to-weight ratio. General von Senger und Etterlin
recommended that future commanders remove all vehicles incapable of coping with mud to an area where
the *rasputiza* was not a factor and to distribute those
vehicles that could maneuver in mud to various units
along the line of march.[31]

To counter the mud, the Germans made organiza-
tional changes and improvements in transportation. One
of the best methods for negotiating the *rasputiza* was the
short, sturdy *panje* horses. In fact, "German mobility
during the spring mud season, by contrast, depended to
a great extent on peasant *panje* wagons."[32] The Soviets
and the Germans used the one-horse *panje* wagon, which
was light enough to ride over the mud without being stuck
carrying small loads of 100–150 kilograms.[33] These
horses were indispensable, and no agency of the German military in the Soviet Union was without them, including the Luftwaffe.[34] The Germans placed many transportation requirements on the "small native *panje* horses
because only they could master the terrain . . . and *panje*
horses could pull through practically anything."[35]

Panje horses, however, despite their ability to negotiate mud, succumbed to the weights they hauled just
like Western-bred horses. Historian Dennis Showalter
wrote that when the Germans faced the *rasputiza* for the
first time, the stress of "hauling guns and wagons through
the mud" proved too much for their Western-bred horses,
even more so for the smaller *panje* horses.[36] Another historian, R. L. DiNardo, stated that when fully provisioned,
the German 105mm artillery piece "weighed as much as
4 tons—[moving it was] a difficult task for six well-fed
heavy draft horses. The standard German Army horse-
drawn vehicle was made of steel, which also proved too
heavy for the small *panje* horses."[37]

A notorious weather system that brings large amounts of seasonal mud is the monsoon. The word "monsoon," derived from the Arabic word for season—*mausin*, applies principally to the "seasonal reversal of pressure and winds over land-masses and neighboring oceans."[38] Although Arabs coined the term, it was in Southeast Asia that the monsoon reigned. Monsoons are predictable, but as Scott Gilmore, an American serving with the Gurkhas as an officer, observed, "the annual rainfall in New York or London is something like 35 inches," while in Assam "400 inches may fall, almost all of it within a period of two and a half months."[39]

Large-scale warfare in Southeast Asia forced strategic planners to give much greater thought to the monsoon than the Germans gave the *rasputiza* in 1941. Just as the *rasputiza* did not take sides, working for and against the Germans and the Soviets, the monsoon in Burma was an ally and a foe to those who fought there. General Slim, planning to remove his troops from Burma in 1942, expressed three fears. The first and most apparent was of the Japanese army, while the second was that he would not be able to keep his army supplied. His third fear was of the monsoon— "the worst danger of all" —for if it came while his army was still trying to escape Burma to the comparative safety of India, then "vehicles would be bogged, and all movement practically impossible. Immobilized, we should be in imminent danger of starving. Even a heavy shower or two might have disastrous consequences." General Slim felt he could avoid the Japanese, logistical failures, or the monsoon but not all three. As it turned out, the Japanese struck Slim's command first, but the monsoon arrived soon thereafter. Consequently, British and Commonwealth troops continued their retreat as best they could, "ploughing their way up slopes, over a track inches

deep in slippery mud." These factors hindered the
British retreat, but also slowed the Japanese pursuit.[40]

As the fortunes of the British Fourteenth Army
changed and the Allies began planning their return to
Burma, General Slim had to consider the monsoon in his
plans. Although he had aircraft, the monsoon's mud hindered his ability to use them. Obviously, the monsoon's
rain-filled skies and heavy clouds were hazards to pilots
in the air, but only all-weather fields could handle take-
offs and landings. In the spring of 1944, the Allies had
only two all-weather airfields, Imphal and Palel, and the
British did not have time to construct any more before
the monsoon's predicted arrival in May.[41] The loss of
grass fields to monsoon rains not only hindered the Fourteenth Army's conventional forces but portended disastrous possibilities for the Chindits—an unconventional
force operating behind Japanese lines. The army depended on air assets to serve as artillery and for resupply. Their largest organic, indirect weapons, those that
did not point or aim straight at the target but rather used
elevation to "lob" shots on the target were mortars. General Slim recalled that mud put the Chindits' grass fields
out of action and diminished the hope of recovering the
sick and wounded.[42] Believing that "a normal monsoon
would break somewhere about the 15th May," he decided, in the spring of 1945, that speed was essential for
his army's advance, which needed a mechanized force
leading the way. As he wrote in *Defeat into Victory*, "it
would be a race, and a stern one, against two tough com-
petitors, the enemy and the monsoon." Slim knew that
he had to reach a major port in South Burma, preferably
Rangoon, which would allow his army to receive supplies and replacements during the monsoon. If not, the
British Fourteenth Army had to have more than one all-
weather road capable of bearing numerous supply col-
umns. However, on May 1, 1945, the monsoon arrived,

weeks earlier than expected, halting the British advance. Within a day, airstrips were out of action, bridges collapsed, and soldiers "slipped, splashed, and skidded forward." Unfortunately, one of Slim's divisions came to a halt 41 miles short of its goal.[43]

As mud affected General Slim's air assets, it also hampered the progress of grass airfields and the engineers that built them throughout most of the South and Central Pacific. The need for airfields capable of withstanding mud's hazards has stretched from aviation's beginnings to the more recent conflict in Kosovo. The Allies, fighting in World War II's Pacific Theater, needed dependable air assets to support their operations. Carrier-based aviation was available but could not provide all the aircraft necessary for victory. Thus, one of the first objectives after securing a beachhead was to develop a local airfield, and accomplishing this mission was the overriding goal of the 808th Engineer Aviation Battalion. Unlike their European Theater counterparts who contended with periods of prolonged wet weather, engineer aviation units in the Pacific Theater learned how to build airfields around monsoons. The 808th constructed airfields in several locations, but projects on New Guinea and Leyte Islands were two of their most important. An essential tool to the accomplishment of the 808th's mission was perforated steel plating also known as Marsden matting. When linked together, these prefabricated metal planks formed sturdy sheets. With holes punched in them to allow water and mud to seep through, the matting provided enough stability for aircraft to land, often on muddy unstable soils. Perforated steel plating also helped patch roads.[44]

The leaders of American operations in the Philippines and on Okinawa did not fully consider the influence of the monsoon or the predictable rainy season of an island at the monsoon's edge. Although the monsoon technically reaches as far as 60 degrees north latitude, monsoon conditions diminish further from the equator.[45] The Philippine Islands were at the northern limits of a monsoon climate, and although Okinawa existed just beyond a monsoon climate, it received monsoon-like conditions.

The Americans knew that Okinawa had a rainy season but did not give it the consideration that the Japanese did. Col. Yahara Hiromichi, the planner of Japan's defensive strategy for Okinawa, understood the rainy season's power and acted accordingly, noting, "we had been waiting for the rains because enemy tanks could not move well in the mud." However, Colonel Yahara did not predict accurately the exact beginning of the rainy season; and, in 1945, it came at the end of May, two weeks later than predicted.[46] Unfortunately for the Japanese, Colonel Yahara also misjudged the rainy season's effect on the Americans. The mud he counted on to hinder the Americans as they advanced was so excessive that it prevented them from advancing at all, an element critical in his plans for having Japanese units retreat before the Americans, then turn and attack them. Consequently, the mud created by the spring rains was such that "the offensive action of enemy tanks, planes, and ships was so slowed by Okinawa's heavy rains that we were getting concerned as to whether the Sixty-second Division's retreat-and-attack plan would be successful."[47]

Regions outside of tropical monsoon areas also have predictable periods of wet weather or local rainy seasons. Italy is one such area. Adding to the description of Italy's rainy season, an American field artillery battalion officer noted that although the battalion received some indirect fire, "routine life began to settle in along with the rain and mud, as it was now November, the peak of the rainy season."[48] In the spring of 1945, the Allied commander of the Italian campaign, Field Marshal Harold

Alexander, decided to wait until the weather improved before destroying what remained of German forces.[49]

Wherever steep grades and water-soaked soils combine, landslides become a hazard. Although unpredictable unless triggered deliberately, landslides occur frequently during monsoons and rainy seasons. Mud affects military operations when combatants, animals, or vehicles move (or attempt to move) through mud, but in the case of landslides, mud *acts* to hinder mobility. When such various factors as soil type, slope, vegetative cover, and amount of soil moisture reach optimal conditions, landslides develop. However, once the land (frequently mud) moves, it often remains in place until someone removes it.[50]

Soldiers under monsoon conditions, such as those in Burma, encountered these obstacles more frequently, although landslides did occur in many places during World War II. General Slim, writing about Southeast Asia's Ledo Road, considered that its construction was a wonderful engineering achievement, but he believed that the real feat came when engineers struggled with several

During the rainy season in Vietnam, troops use laterite to stabilize a road south of Can Tho in April 1967. *Ivyl Myers*

large landslides created by the rains. Burma's monsoon in July 1944 caused great difficulty for the Fourteenth Army. Entire chunks of roads vital for moving the army disappeared as slopes turned to mud and lost their resistance to the soil's weight.[51] Scott Gilmore noted after exceptionally bad weather that "the tracks up and down the mountains were washed out, became mud slides."[52] During the fall of 1944, a medical company with the American Thirty-fourth Infantry Division in Italy had numerous difficulties with slides, forcing the unit to use its Italian litter bearers to clear the debris.[53]

Monsoons and predictable rainy seasons produce large quantities of slippery mud that soldiers must deal with. Describing the situation in late May 1944, General Slim recalled how the fighting in southern Burma became a stalemate caused by the enemy's defense and "the extreme difficulty of movement on these slippery, steep jungle slopes." Slippery mud also delayed essential supplies because the supply road for one of General Slim's divisions was "a 12-mile twisting ribbon of mud along which jeeps skidded and slithered, their wheels spinning."[54]

U.S. Marine E. B. Sledge remembered that the arrival of the spring rains and his numerous encounters with slippery mud began with ten days of monsoon-like rain. "The weather was chilly and mud, mud, mud was everywhere," causing him to lose his balance with nearly every step he took on the trail. He compared his descent down a muddy slope, after repelling a Japanese assault, to "trying to walk down a greased slide." Sledge explained how difficult slippery mud was for the movement of an entire unit, when he described how his unit slipped and slid along hillsides covered with mud. The problem was that if only one marine slipped and fell, he could take numerous others down with him.[55]

Not only was the terrain tricky for Sledge, it was difficult for the Japanese as well. Sledge considered this as he waited for Japanese infiltrators who never appeared, believing, "the Japanese simply couldn't crawl up the slick surface."[56] Colonel Yahara added, "The muddy roads were slippery. It was difficult to walk. As we squished through the mud, I could not believe the Sixty-second Division was retreating under such conditions."[57] L.Cpl. Kojima Masao, retreating from Burma in 1945, remembered how he climbed mountains with heavy loads making the move difficult as he slipped and sank in the mud.[58]

During the Vietnam War, American military planners attempted to use seasonal mud to their advantage. They intended to target the Ho Chi Minh trail, a network of routes that provided "Communist forces in South Vietnam with one-fourth of all their supplies (more than 70 percent of arms and munitions)."[59] Southeast Asia's monsoons forced logistical movement along the trail to vary with the conditions. From April until October, the southwest monsoon made mobility along it very inefficient. North Vietnamese planners, who understood this predictable, natural condition, moved supplies to staging positions until the trail dried. The Americans observed that the monsoon placed Communist forces in South Vietnam in a difficult position while they waited for supplies to resume. If the flow of supplies into South Vietnam at that time could be severely limited, attacks against American and South Vietnamese targets would diminish, if not stop altogether. Therefore, American forces developed Operation Plan (OPLAN) El Paso and Project Popeye to use the timing of the monsoon to their advantage.

The U.S. Army developed OPLAN El Paso to disrupt the Ho Chi Minh Trail's flow of supplies. For the proposed operation to work, Army personnel had to understand the dichotomy of monsoon conditions in Southeast Asia. The launching point for all operations and airstrikes considered in the plan was South Vietnam, a land wet with monsoon rains for part of the year, while the intended area of operations, Laos, was dry. At other times of the year, Laos would have its monsoon season while South Vietnam was dry. The best time to begin the proposed operation was in November as the northeast monsoon ended but before the trail dried too significantly for the North Vietnamese to reconstitute their forces in the South. The plan acknowledged a predictable seasonal event and intended to use it.[60]

But as American planners proposed to use the monsoon against the North Vietnamese, they also had to consider its effects against U.S. forces conducting OPLAN El Paso. It was to be a corps-level operation requiring significant logistical support and an all-weather supply route. The only option was Route 9, which ran through northern South Vietnam. However, the original asphalt surface of Route 9 was less than 1 inch thick, and by the late 1960s, very little of it existed. The mud, intended to slow the North Vietnamese, would also hinder the Americans, as the "glutinous gumbo" might play havoc with their supply operations. The planned operation was never implemented.[61]

Another proposed American strike at the Ho Chi Minh Trail was through Project Popeye, "a clandestine, all-service military/civilian program."[62] The intent of Project Popeye was to create more mud and seriously erode North Vietnam's ability to move supplies and personnel along the trail. Intelligence sources monitoring movement discovered that during the transition period between the northeast monsoon and the southwest monsoon (April to mid-May) "even isolated thunderstorms temporarily interrupted logistic operations."[63] The Joint Chiefs of Staff agreed that an increase in rainfall during and after the typical monsoon season would prove most beneficial to South Vietnam's defense. Therefore, the U.S. Navy received orders to begin operational testing.[64]

The U.S. military intended to extend precipitation through cloud seeding until the end of June when the southwest monsoon returned and soil moisture turned the trail into a soggy mess.[65]

The project had two goals. The first was to "increase rainfall sufficiently in carefully selected target areas to further soften the road surfaces and cause landslides along roadways." The second goal was to keep the soil surface in the target area saturated beyond the monsoon's regular period.[66] The test area for Project Popeye was the southeastern corner of Laos, an area "criss-crossed by infiltration routes from the north," where even moderate amounts of precipitation were detrimental to poorly built trails and roads. The test area "experienced northeasterly winds and a relatively dry season from November to March and southwesterly winds and a rainy season from April to October."[67] Assessing the results of the cloud seeding project proved difficult. Radar provided the military with adequate estimates of the amount of precipitation, but because the target area was a war zone, results were unreliable.[68]

Thus, the project's success was based on determining if any increased precipitation was because of human intervention or the natural effects of the monsoon. In 1982, E. M. Frisby, a project scientist, remarked on how difficult it was to measure the resulting rainfall accurately because of the operation's "lack of ground precipitation data, and by the many gaps in the various synoptic observational networks."[69] In the final report, scientists felt confident "that judicious seeding of properly selected clouds resulted in remarkably increased cloud growth relative to the growth that would have occurred naturally." They concluded that increased rainfall from cloud seeding affected military traffic on the trail.[70]

In addition, taking estimates of increased rainfall from as high as 30 percent to as low as 15 percent, Frisby believed that these values demonstrated "appreciable precipitation increases in areas of naturally heavy rain."[71] However, the information garnered did not determine if the project was tactically sound enough to show a military impact, only that it was operationally feasible.[72] Despite knowing that increased rainfall along the trail was possible, "its results were declared quantitatively inconclusive."[73] Col. Harry E. "Ed" Soyster, in an appearance before the U.S. Senate, did provide one piece of statistical information proving that the project was tactically viable. Remote sensors detected, at the beginning of April 1971, "[more than] 9,000 enemy logistic movers per week in eastern Laos. By the end of June this number was [fewer] than 900." However, Soyster admitted that typhoons Anna and Frieda, and tropical storm Golda, all struck the area in June 1971. He stated,that only in Southeast Aisa, because of its unique climate, could cloud seeding have produced more mud. He also admitted that the project might have never commenced were it not for the primitive nature of the Ho Chi Minh Trail. Increased rainfall would only influence primitive road conditions such as those found in the target area. Cloud seeding operations in Southeast Asia lasted from March 1967 until July 1972, when journalist Jack Anderson exposed the project in March 1971, and the public outcry became great enough that "the UN general assembly approved a universal treaty banning environmental warfare."[74]

CHAPTER 4

Random Mud

"Mud is the greatest enemy of the armored division."[1]
—*F. M. von Senger und Etterlin*

In December 1941, Gen. George S. Patton Jr. prayed for better weather. Patton's plea mentioned that "rain, snow, more rain, more snow" were factors that worked against the Americans, and he openly questioned God, "Whose side are You on, anyway?" Patton needed clear skies for aircraft to bomb and strafe and spot for artillery, but he needed the sun for another reason so he closed his prayer with this essential request: "Give me four days to dry out this blasted mud."[2]

Random mud appears when storms and sudden thaws increase the amount of moisture in the soil. It appears within minutes and can change the battlefield from a powdery dust into a sticky quagmire, and the transitory nature of random mud has caught even the greatest commanders unprepared. Few excuses exist for military commanders surprised by permanent or seasonal mud. However, mud that arrives after a long powerful thunderstorm, after a few days of steady rain, or from a thaw created by a great surge of warm temperatures can "muddy up" a commander's intended offensive. Random mud's unpredictability means that the timetable for an attack can alter considerably in the space of a few hours, and with it, the difference between success and failure. In its physical composition, random mud does not differ from permanent and seasonal mud. However, Type I mud occurs less often in random mud because significant amounts of moisture—not always available from sudden storms—are necessary for bottomless mud. This chapter, using the battles of the Reichswald, Kursk, and Waterloo as examples, examines random mud generated by summer storms and thaws, and the subsequent postponement of battles.

An excellent source of random mud is summer storms. However, these meteorological events do not always create enough mud, Type I particularly, to hinder military operations. Additionally, isolated storms associated with continental interiors are not always great enough to cover an entire battlefield, a situation more apparent in the large conventional battles of World Wars I and II. Random occurrences of mud exasperate commanders who often overlook its influence and assume consistent conditions over an entire operational area.

The random appearance of mud in North Africa saved the Afrika Korps from a further drubbing after El Alamein. Permanent mud, the kind present in the salt marshes of the Qattara Depression, prevented the Afrika Korps from flanking Allied positions at El Alamein, forcing them to assault the British Eighth Army. The British force blunted the Axis assault and then launched its own offensive driving the Germans and Italians back toward Libya. However, mud from a sudden storm altered the situation. Gen. Sir Brian Horrocks recalled that the rain caused the desert to "become quite impassable for wheeled and tracked vehicles." Generally, when rain fell across a battlefield, the mud hindered both sides, but in this instance, the Afrika Korps already had access to an all-weather road and continued its withdrawal. Horrocks observed that, "The [British] First Armoured Division was practically within sight of the vital desert road," yet, along with two other divisions, it "might have been stuck in glue" and the British made no substantial gains for three days. A similar situation occurred later in the offensive when the British "Seventh Armoured Division was almost in a position to block the escape route" and more rain-induced mud intervened to stop the British— but not the Germans—from moving along a permanent road.[3]

Before encountering the *rasputiza*, the Germans discovered how random summer rains destroyed Russian roads. In July 1941, as the Germans were about to encircle a large pocket of Soviet troops, heavy rains provided enough mud to slow the German advance to only a few hours a day and allowed two hundred thousand Soviet soldiers to escape capture.[4] In June 1942, rains hindered the progress of the German advance across the Ukraine, but at the end of the month, heavy rains created mud so impassable that at least two mechanized divisions' advance elements had to leave their vehicles and continue their advance toward Stalingrad on foot.[5]

In the Battle of Kursk, mud was more a significant factor than many historians admit. The advancing Germans, trying to cut off the Kursk salient, halted "in the midst of heavy thunderstorms that turned the battlefield into a sea of mud."[6] German planners who launched the offensive in early July 1943 did not concern themselves with mud because the *rasputiza* did not occur in the summer. Instead, they looked back at their successful offensives in the Soviet Union and concluded that launching an offensive had a better chance of success in late June. For example, the early stages of Operation Barbarossa and the Blau offensive were successful operations launched in late June 1941 and June 1942.[7]

Significant to the encounter's outcome was the soil type and soil moisture content of the battlefield. The Kursk region was famous for its black earth, which was "extremely fine, producing considerable dust when dry and then dissolving into a muddy morass after a rain."[8] For example, one of the principle tank battles occurred near Prokhorovka where Soviet Gen. Pavel A. Rotmistrov knew of the soil conditions. The land "dried easily and quickly. . . . It would throw huge dust clouds into the air and might well isolate the battlefield from heavy air support, once the tanks were engaged."[9] The Battle of Kursk provided a rare look at an offensive where the soil moisture content moved from one extreme to another with both elements playing a role in the battle. The length of the engagement, the warm temperatures of early summer, and the number of troops and vehicles involved meant that although the area started extremely dry, the offensive stalled in a quagmire after a line of thunderstorms moved through. Days later, the soil moisture content fell low enough for dust clouds to develop.

The battle commenced under the weather conditions that German meteorologists had forecast, but conditions later turned disastrous when heavy summer rains turned the dust to mud. The weather of late June and early July cooperated enough for forecasters to predict a sunny day for German air assets. However, the weather began to change on the salient's southern sector during the night of July 4 when thunderstorms unleashed torrents of rain. As the Germans tried to advance, "the earth turned into a thick quagmire. Especially between Ssyrzw and Sawidowka did the earth disappear into a bog." On the next day, further complications meant delays for the

German offensive when speed was essential. For instance, the thunderstorms that erupted on the evening of July 4 caused one German division a great deal of difficulty. A muddy quagmire and a river to its front, overflowing its banks, turned the floodplain "into a great swamp." Soviet artillery, taking advantage of the rain and the darkness, set up on the opposite side of the river and prepared to take a severe toll on the immobile German division.

As mud gripped the German tanks, Soviet commanders allowed their ground attack fighters to strike German tanks wherever they were in the greatest concentrations. The mud had left German armor "largely immobile, thus becoming excellent targets."[10] "The roads were muddy and mostly impassable except for horses and cross-country vehicles. The muddy conditions delayed activity on the ground, and the rain reduced the number of planes in the air," according to Walter S. Dunn Jr.'s *Kursk: Hitler's Gamble, 1943*.[11]

On July 11, an assault by a German armored division failed to launch on time as the abysmal roads complicated the movement of artillery and delayed the attack by 45 minutes.[12] Despite having a bridge capable of handling the heavy Tiger tanks necessary for the offensive, any "advance from the bridgehead was made impossible by the heavy rain. Nothing could move on the ground except tanks, and the Luftwaffe could not fly."[13]

As the offensive continued, rain-induced mud hampered the southern sector of the German offensive. The rain that fell near Prokhorovka was not heavy enough to halt operations, but as the day progressed, "heavier showers turned many of the roads into muddy quagmires," especially where the Soviet Second Guards Tank Corps intended to operate.[14] Although the mud was not deep enough to stop tracked vehicles from maneuvering, Dunn wrote that the Germans found it hard to stop the attack of the Soviet Fifty-first and Fifty-second Rifle Divisions "because the muddy roads immobilized the German munitions trucks creating a shortage of artillery shells."[15] The day broke overcast on July 14, but it did not rain. The sun eventually rose and began drying the roads and making them accessible for all vehicles, but the German offensive had lost its momentum by this date and good weather favored the Soviets as it freed their air assets.[16]

The thawing of snow is a seasonal factor, but it can be random as well. In areas where snowfall is significant, commanders know the snow will melt and mud will accompany it. However, in the heart of winter an unexpected increase in temperatures, often combined with rain, plentiful sunshine, or warmer winds brings sudden thaws with disastrous consequences for some military operations. This happened in the Battle of the Reichswald. Conversely, mud causes a different set of difficulties when it freezes. When soil moisture falls to the freezing point, it often acts like concrete, greatly enhancing mud's suctioning effect.

Thaws do not always occur in spring, and even strong sunlight can cause a local thaw. If the temperature increases enough, a thaw can occur in January. German soldier Gottlob Bidermann wrote how a mid-January thaw disintegrated roads into muddy quagmires. He witnessed how soldiers harnessed motorized vehicles to teams of horses. "The reliable animals were often able to make slow but deliberate headway through the mud, the mechanized transports remained helplessly mired in place."[17] In addition, strong sunlight could heat the ground enough to allow heavy tanks such as the German Tiger to sink "so deeply into the marshy ground that they were practically sitting on their hulls."[18]

In early February 1945, an unexpected thaw struck British and Commonwealth soldiers fighting in the Reichswald. The British commander Gen. Sir Brian Horrocks remembered how mud cost him a smooth and easy victory. For his plan to attack the Reichswald and cross the Rhine River, he needed surprise and the weather's cooperation. Horrocks also needed the ground to remain frozen until at least February 9, 1945, thus allowing tanks and supply vehicles to move cross-country independent of roads.[19] However, a few days before launching the assault, rain fell and induced a thaw.

Mud was unusual in early February. Consequently, the British did not seriously consider the effect of a major rain-induced thaw, a notion that Horrocks reaffirmed when he related how his staff responded well when the "thaw set in and the bottom literally dropped out of several vital roads."[20] Horrocks felt that despite the

Combat engineers dig out a bulldozer struck in a muddy bomb crater near Marigny, France, in July 1944. *U.S. Army Military History Institute*

numerous forces provided for the offensive, his plan was not unreasonable; "what was not given due allowance though was the very bad state of the roads."[21]

The thaw was the source of Horrocks's difficulties largely because the British had only one heavy-duty road. Historian Peter Elstob observed that other than this one hard-surface road, the British had only single lane unsurfaced forest roads. "The roads were going to have to carry many times the traffic they had been built to bear and as long as the temperature remained below freezing this was quite possible—for a short period." However, when the thaw-induced mud appeared before the battle started, all the secondary roads failed.[22]

The mud hindered British preparations and handicapped the attack. When the assault began, mine-clearing flail tanks floundered and "the start line was soon jammed with bogged vehicles."[23] Horrocks reported, "It was so bad that after the first hour every tank going across country was bogged down, and the infantry had to struggle forward on their own."[24] The British used engineers and bulldozers to fix the worst spots and sent Churchill tanks to "prove" routes and create new ones in the forests.[25] The thaw-induced mud destroyed several infantry-armor attacks. Sherman tanks and variants built on the Sherman's chassis failed to negotiate the mud, and many mired in the first few hundred yards of their assault points. The Fifteenth Scottish Division began the battle with limited armor support because the tanks attached to it bogged in the mud. In addition, Elstob hinted that several members of the Highland Light Infantry died needlessly in a minefield because the flail tanks, which had bogged in the mud, failed to neutralize the mines.[26] As the roads collapsed, the offensive slowed. On the assault's second day, traffic on many roads ceased while engineers tried to repair them. By February 11, 1945, the roads were so bad that tanks had to stay off the main road, which continued to deteriorate because the movement of essential supply vehicles prevented any attempts at repairing it.[27]

Horrocks achieved the necessary surprise, but mud cost him the quick victory he desired. After the war he wrote,

> The thaw had been a great blow, because in front of us in the low-lying valley the going was certain to be bad. Luckily for my peace of mind I did not realize then just how bad. The main trouble was mines—and mud, particularly mud. What was so maddening was that the whole thing could have been so easy if only the frost had continued. Instead of the lovely hard frozen "going," we were faced by oceans of mud and water and within ten minutes of the start every tank—in fact every vehicle—was bogged down.[28]

He added that the mud was so overwhelming that after the battle began generals played no significant role, as the fight became a slugfest in the mud.[29]

Frozen mud sometimes was all an offensive needed to regain momentum after struggling through quagmires; but, on a smaller scale, frozen mud could also bind. For instance, one German soldier working on defensive positions in 1944 found that his "work was interrupted abruptly in mid-December by a deep, sudden frost. The earth froze to the consistency of stone," but the formerly impassable roads were then hard enough to handle traffic. Although the *panje* horses proved most beneficial to the Germans and Soviets during World War II, they needed close attention. Bidermann found, after a freezing night in the Crimea, that the animals he was responsible for had "their front hooves frozen fast in the deep mud. It was necessary to hack them free with a pick."[30]

Some combatants discovered a few important lessons for operating in conditions when the mud froze at night and then thawed in the day. General von Senger und Etterlin, writing about the tribulations his panzer division experienced while moving between sectors of the Eastern Front, recalled that the real difficulties for the division came after the first night, when the temperature fell below freezing and ruts hardened as the water in the saturated soil froze. Freezing mud also enclosed those vehicles that bogged down during the day. One solution for retrieving them was to wait until the mud thawed, making it possible to snatch them from the mud, but another alternative was to blow them out of the mud with explosives. To retrieve mired vehicles, the Germans left their towed artillery pieces and used the tractors that hauled them to pull other vehicles from the mud. Once out of the mud the Germans formed convoys by hooking a series of less mobile vehicles to one capable of

Chinese and Americans pull a C-47 out of the mud in June 1945. *National Archives*

negotiating the soft soil. Taking advantage of the frozen mud before it thawed in the early morning was a hard-won lesson. To facilitate the use of the frozen mud and rid themselves of the extensive ruts that immobilized fully tracked vehicles, the Germans learned to block off sections of road to keep them smooth and passable when frozen.[31]

U.S. Marines fighting in Korea learned how mud changed between night and day in February 1951. When the sun set and temperatures fell, the broken muddy ground froze to something resembling concrete, but when day broke, the sun thawed the frozen soil into Type IIb mud which made walking difficult. As Maj. Allan Bevilacqua noted, the marines repeatedly pulled each foot from the suctioning mud and "negotiated the mire with the exaggerated high-kneed gait of a drunk staggering his way through a pasture, all the while trying to keep from stepping into anything."[32]

Many commanders, when suddenly facing large quantities of mud and knowing that it hinders movement and softens artillery effectiveness, tend to postpone offensive actions. Conversely, often when mud dried on World War I's Western Front, new offensives would commence. In some instances postponing operations because of mud proved beneficial and on at least one occasion the decision to postpone a battle because of mud ended in defeat. When mud dries and soil moisture returns to a normal state, commanders plan based on the belief that the terrain regains some measure of consistency.

Commanders know that soldiers, horses, and wagons move better after the mud dries. In March 1865, Gen. Ulysses S. Grant had to wait until the mud from heavy winter rains dried sufficiently to move his wagons and cannons, although he wanted very much to attack Gen.

Robert E. Lee's army and end the war. At the same time, General Lee also waited for the mud to dry for his evacuation of locations not worth holding.[33] Even commanders such as the vilified Field Marshal Sir Douglas Haig sometimes saw the futility of ordering battle when the ground did not permit it. In August 1918, the conditions were so bad that "operations of any magnitude became impossible, and the resumption of our offensive was necessarily postponed until a period of fine weather would allow the ground to recover." However, Haig believed that the mud-induced delay "was of the greatest service to the enemy."[34] During World War II's Italian campaign, Lt. Gen. E. L. M. Burns noted how random mud delayed an operation in May 1944 when an unexpected rain "turned the sandy tracks bulldozed along the valley into mud."[35]

Sunny skies and warm winds did provide commanders with new opportunities to attack. Stretcher bearer Frank Dunham observed that, in January 1918, an appearance by the sun caused the mud to dry. However, as the sun brightened his spirits, it also helped to continue the war. "The fine weather was the signal for warfare to begin again, and the German gunners got busy shelling the roadway close by us."[36] Military geographer Douglas Johnson wrote that local battles occurred almost daily, but "every time the sun or a favorable wind dried the ground even a little, new assaults on a larger scale were attempted."[37] Lieutenant General Burns, remembering one reason why the fighting around Amiens worked better in 1918 than earlier, observed how the lack of mud, which had dried in the clear weather, meant that the ground remained in good enough condition to handle traffic insteaad of becoming an expanse of craters churned to mud by artillery.[38] Henry Metelmann recalled how the commander of the German Sixth Army, Gen. Friedrich Paulus, waited for the mud to dry after summer storms. With his patience, the Sixth Army never gained "less than 30 kilometers a day."[39]

The French lost the Battle of Waterloo for various reasons, but one factor that few historians emphasize was random mud's influence. Napoleon Bonaparte lost the battle when Prussian reinforcements, led by Field Marshal Gebhard von Blücher, arrived late in the day while the battle was still in progress and could still be influenced. The reason the battle "ran late" was that Napoleon had postponed the initial morning attack hoping a few additional hours would allow the battlefield's mud to dry.

Napoleon believed that mud and the actions of some key subordinates influenced the battle. After the Battle of Quatre Bras, two days before the Waterloo battle, Napoleon erupted when he found Marshal Michel Ney's soldiers eating rather than pursuing the Duke of Wellington's army. In one of the great what ifs of history, David Chandler, a military historian, wrote that Napoleon might have caught Wellington and forced a fight after Quatre Bras had mud not then made a sudden appearance. "At this juncture a colossal thunderstorm burst overhead, and within minutes the ground was turned into a quagmire. This ruled out any moves across country, and the French pursuit was consequently confined to the roads. Even so, it was a close run thing."[40]

The night before Waterloo the rain fell so hard that even Napoleon commented on it. "The rain was falling in torrents. On the roadway the soldiers were halfway up to their knees in water. On the surrounding ground they sank up to their knees. The artillery could not get through, and the cavalry could only get along with difficulty. This made the retreat of the enemy's cavalry difficult."[41] Napoleon, writing in his memoirs years after the battle, remembered that Marshal Emmanuel Grouchy stopped shadowing Blücher the night before Waterloo. "During the night the rain continued to fall, which made all the flat country more or less impassable for artillery, cavalry and even infantry." However, Blücher continued and subsequently put three hours of movement between his forces and Grouchy's. According to Napoleon, "this disastrous resolve is the principle cause of the loss of the battle of Waterloo." In addition, Grouchy told Napoleon by dispatch rider that he intended to pursue Blücher at 2 A.M., but when day broke Grouchy delayed until 10 A.M. The dispatch rider told Napoleon the delay had been caused by the extremely muddy conditions.[42]

Time was the critical element at Waterloo. Napoleon could defeat the Allied forces under either the Duke of Wellington or Field Marshal Blücher, but not both. Although Blücher had a 3-hour head start on Grouchy, when the battle commenced, Blücher discovered that the mud made moving toward the battle difficult. As Napoleon and Wellington's forces used the main roads, Blücher used substandard secondary roads.[43] Napoleon, despite knowing that Blücher had marched toward Wellington and that Grouchy had started his pursuit late, decided to delay the battle's opening on the advice of Gen. Antoine Drouot who counseled that "the ground was still far too wet to allow the guns to maneuver easily or to employ ricochet fire against the enemy." Consequently, Napoleon ordered that the battle begin at 1 P.M., well into the day. Chandler believed that "this decision proved the most fatal one of the day for the French. For had even an inadequately supported infantry attack been launched against Wellington during the morning, the French must surely have won; for Blücher would have been too late arriving on the field to affect the issue."[44]

Not only did mud influence Napoleon's decision to postpone the battle, it also affected the action. The French commenced the battle with a cannonade from their Grande Battery, but it was not effective. Many of

Wellington's soldiers were on the reverse slope, and those who were in range did not suffer as badly as they might have because the mud's dampening effect "prevented the roundshot from ricocheting and the cannonballs were often swallowed up."[45] When the French infantry attacked, maintaining tight orderly formations in the mud was nearly impossible. The Type IIb mud, which caked to their feet, combined with long tough stalks of rye, pulled off their shoes.[46] Mud also hindered Marshal Ney's charge as it reduced the cavalry attack to a less shocking trot.[47] When Napoleon launched the Old Guard near the engagement's end, it contended with mud churned all day by soldiers in formation and assaults made by both sides. The Old Guard slogged through a thousand yards of churned up mud, exposed to artillery fire as they went, and were unable to execute neat maneuvers in column because of the mud.[48]

Napoleon was at the battle, but from his location, he could not see the entire battlefield. Consequently, battle-

Soldiers use an old door to smooth a muddy road in Germany in 1945. *National Archives*

field obstructions, as well as mud and the fatigue it caused the courier's horse, meant that, when Napoleon sent a message, it took the courier 15 minutes to return with a reply. Conversely, Wellington stayed in sight of the battle-field and moved from one location to another shortening the time lag on orders and messages.[49]

CHAPTER 5

Mud and Engineers

"So ended one of the most disastrous months in the entire career of the 808th!! Never had the battalion been so completely stopped by rain and mud."[1]
—*The History of the 808th Engineer Aviation Battalion*

Engineers have a special relationship with mud. Armor, artillery, cavalry, infantry, and other combat arms have experienced mud's dirty tricks but engineers take aim at neutralizing mud. Humans have known for centuries that mud is a useful material for constructing homes and many other projects, especially in arid regions where trees are few and precipitation that might deteriorate a mud-built structure is infrequent. Mud also has a role in creating fortifications. Conversely, combatants construct roads, corduroy roads, and duckboards to defeat the power of mud.

In certain areas of the world, mud forts are common. Such fortifications vary from large stable forts composed of dried mud to smaller, less formidable and more expedient works of wet mud. Although the influence of dried mud on warfare is not the subject of this book, it is worth mentioning a few occurrences. In its earliest phases of construction, the Great Wall of China was of mud-based construction, and a more recent action in Afghanistan occurred at the mud fort of Mazar-e Sharif.[2] British colonial wars in Nepal and New Zealand encountered the power of mud forts, and the seemingly simple fortifications of their Gurkha and Maori opponents used mud's dampening effect to reduce the efficiency of British artillery.

Mud can be either a positive or a negative influence when combatants dig entrenchments. On the positive side, soft soil with minimal moisture content—while barely meeting the average citizen's definition of mud—is a blessing to those infantrymen digging for their lives and is even easier if a shovel (a necessary piece of equipment for ground combatants) is available. Marine E. B. Sledge noted that his mortar crew dug a very good gun pit after their initial landing on Okinawa because the soft soil made for easy shoveling. In *The Men of Company K*, the authors stated that the soldier's entrenching tool was second only to the M-1 Garand rifle as a valuable possession. Under fire, soldiers often found themselves with only a bayonet, helmet, mess kit, or short-handled entrenching tool for digging, and more often than not, they must dig from a prone position. One American soldier in World War II remembered losing his shovel when given orders to dig in, but being a practical man, he used his steel helmet on the muddy ground.[3]

Conversely, mud is also an impediment to constructing and maintaining entrenchments. At times, Type II mud is a hindrance as Type IIb's adhesiveness makes digging tiresome, while the liquid nature of Type IIa threatens some entrenchments with collapse. In the static warfare of World War I's Western Front, the future Field Marshal Rommel received his first taste of battle and learned the value of digging. Rommel recounted an instance in which French artillery began falling thick and heavy. His men, avoiding the detrimental consequences of the collision of artillery and its collateral effects with human flesh, dug deep into the earth. The soldiers found the digging difficult because of the clay coating that stuck to their shovel blades. Rommel knew that "work progressed very slowly in the wet, clayey soil. Over and over, shovels became coated with a thick, sticky coat of clay and had to be cleaned."[4] Too much Type IIa mud also causes great difficulties in digging entrenchments. In January 1945, the U.S. Army's 133rd Infantry Regiment contended with mud from melting and shifting snow that "threatened to cave in foxholes, dugouts, and gun emplacements. Front liners in many instances had to reinforce their positions with sandbags, shell casings, and wood."[5] During the Vietnam War, Type IIa mud made digging a useless venture. Patrols sent out during the

Seventh Army engineers laid planks over this muddy road in France that had broken up under heavy military traffic. *U.S. Military History Institute*

dry season dug fighting positions when they halted, but often during the monsoon, patrol leaders were known to forego fighting positions, deeming such digging as an exercise in futility.[6]

Roads are crucial to successful offensives and good all-weather roads are essential in muddy areas. Not until the twentieth century have roads proliferated throughout the world's industrialized regions, and reliable roads are even less frequent in Asia, Africa, and South America. Paved roads are best at absorbing high levels of abuse from soldiers and their equipment.

Permanent roads factor significantly in campaigns because the military force capable of utilizing solid roads does not have to flounder in the muddy tracks that were once dirt roads. German tank commander Otto Carius knew the value of paved highways. While fighting the Allies in western Germany, he stated that the Americans were surely grateful to Hitler for the autobahn. "If only we had found such roads during our advance into Russia! We then would have reached Moscow and not have remained stuck in the mud."[7] However, what appeared to be a good road could turn quickly into a quagmire when abused by heavy military traffic. Truck convoys, thundering down roads of fragile construction, proved disastrous to France's thin roads during World War I. General Herringham remembered that frost and heavy traffic destroyed their thin surface, especially those segments covering areas of chalk. The frost, penetrating through the road's crust, turned any moisture below the surface to ice. The water, expanding as it froze, "crushed the chalk into powder." No apparent signs of damage existed until the frost thawed, causing the underlying chalk to turn to oatmeal. The road's surface, "no longer supported on a solid foundation, broke and sank into it, while the chalky pulp below burst through forming a morass." Herringham explained that the military relied on such roads for supplies, and as the mud and traffic increased, these roads ceased to exist. Eventually, military authorities stopped all nonessential traffic while major repairs began.[8]

The need for good roads can force some commanders to use alternative construction materials. Monsoon-induced mud in Southeast Asia encouraged innovative road construction in Burma and Vietnam. When not enough gravel was available to build an all-weather road through Burma's Arrakan region, Gen. William Slim's engineers used mud to defeat mud, in a sense, by constructing a road with millions of bricks. To supply enough bricks for the intended road, Slim imported India's best brick makers and built kilns approximately every 20 miles, stating "a brick road is terribly apt in rain to sink into the earth, but, constantly having fresh bricks relaid, it held, a monument to ingenuity and determination."

On another occasion, Slim's chief engineer used "bithess" as an all-weather road material. Using hand labor, the engineers packed the earthen road level and tight from Tamu to Kalewa. They used "overlapping strips of Hessian cloth, dipped in bitumen" to build more than 100 critical miles. Until the monsoon's arrival, the road handled hundreds of vehicles every day. In 1967, Lieutenant Myers made great use of laterite—a material similar to clay with "a lot of iron ore." He recalled that laterite was "almost like a gum eraser, not fully soft, but it could be cut, and when dried made good brick material." Myers's engineers dug it out, spread it, rolled it, and made serviceable roads with it.[9]

Engineers, especially those trained for road construction, are the preferred labor source for building thoroughfares, but if they are not available, then ordinary soldiers build roads. During World War II's Battle of the Reichswald, mud and excessive traffic so thoroughly destroyed all avenues of approach that more than eighty engineers and road construction companies worked steadily to build or repair 500 miles of roads.[10] In addition, many soldiers took up picks and shovels to repair roads before their units could advance. During World War II's Italian campaign, the U.S. Army's 631st Field Artillery Battalion used all available materials to build a road for their advance.[11]

Corduroy roads, improvised routes built from logs often at least 10 inches in diameter, are an important method of countering long expanses of mud. These roads permit movement over swamps and large muddy areas but only at low speeds. Wide enough only for one-way traffic but with sideouts built in along certain intervals, corduroy roads are essential for successful military operations in wetlands. In the Soviet Union, the absence of gravel and stone forced German engineers to build miles and miles of corduroy roads, which took a toll on trucks and soldiers and restricted vehicles to rates of advance around 5 miles per hour. Corduroy roads were so important to General Rendulic that he recommended that the necessary logs for building the roads be precut and stacked along the intended route. He felt such planning was most significant in areas of the Soviet Union where trees were scarce, not only because of the obvious lack of material, but also because massive transportation assets were needed to move the logs from areas where trees were more plentiful.[12]

Corduroy roads are essential for supplying forward-deployed soldiers. For sustaining his drive into the Soviet Union, General Guderian recalled the importance of corduroy roads. As his units advanced, they built many miles of corduroy roads to stay continually supplied with the few provisions available.[13] Concerning the Soviet Union's muddy season in October 1941, Siegfried Knappe, a German artillery officer, wrote, "The mud was so bad that nothing could move in it." Corduroy roads were the solution, and Knappe's artillery unit built them from its gun positions to rear area ammunition and supply dumps.[14] In the swamps of northern Russia, the Germans even constructed a corduroy road for a miniature rail system.[15]

Wooden logs are the most common material used to build corduroy roads, but other materials also work well. During World War II's North African campaign, British reconnaissance units with wheeled vehicles carried "sand channels," which were "long steel strips, reinforced underneath, about 16 feet long," using them to cross muddy areas. Myers used corduroy roads when his construction sites grew too muddy, often using whole logs rather than splitting them. However, he also learned a new road-building system for countering mud's characteristics and effects from a unit of South Vietnamese engineers. The South Vietnamese cut banana fronds, laid them out in a herringbone manner, and placed laterite over the fronds. They then put another layer of banana fronds in a herringbone style, but in a different direction atop the first layer, placing more laterite on top. The two groups of engineers, continuing until they constructed four such layers, then waited for the material to dry. Myers described the road as a "semi-floating almost flexible dirt bridge that took a lot of fronds and laterite." The improvised road supported 2½-ton trucks, towed artillery pieces, and lasted four days with only minor repairs.[16]

Wooden walkways or duckboards are smaller scale versions of corduroy roads. Duckboards allow soldiers in trenches and siege lines a reprieve from the excessively muddy conditions that occur in static warfare. The muddy conditions of World War I trenches required the construction of wooden paths to keep soldiers from sinking into muddy areas, some of which were very deep. A duckboard was the subject of one soldier's poem written about World War I's Western Front.

Walking one day on a duckboard.
I was weary and ill at ease,
And my hands grasped vainly at nothing,
And the mud came up to my knees,
The duckboard began oscillating,
I knew that I had to go,
So I gave one wild and final lunge,
And I fell in the mud below.[17]

Burns, remembering his experiences at Passchendaele, wrote, "there were endless duckboard tracks, winding erratically towards the front. To leave them was to sink into a slough."[18] Guy Sajer recalled one occasion in the Soviet Union when guards stood on "empty munitions cases. . . so the sentry wouldn't sink in the mud."[19]

Duckboards are a convenience for soldiers enduring muddy conditions, but in certain situations they are essential for operations. Rendulic, when describing positional warfare in the Soviet Union, wrote after World War II that duckboards were a necessity because mud made trenches difficult to traverse.[20] Not all methods of keeping soldiers from trench mud are as good. Frank Dunham recalled how fellow soldiers tried to make their going easier through knee-deep mud by placing "bits of wood and tin into the mud, making a few dry stepping places,"[21] and Sajer remembered one occasion when large amounts of Type IIa mud swallowed the stones he and a friend thought might improve a path. During World War II, Bill Mauldin observed that many American soldiers used cardboard shellcases for building corduroy walkways and Evans recalled the frequent use of long planks as walkways in Vietnam.[22]

Duckboards also provide essential stable bases for mortars. The American Ninety-sixth Infantry Division's "After Action Report" for the Philippines campaign had some recommendations concerning 4.2-inch mortars. Although the division believed they were excellent weapons, the muddy conditions limited their role. When these mortars "fired on marshy ground, the base plates would continually sink, causing inaccuracy."[23] Mud forced mortar crews on Guadalcanal "to [resight] tubes pounded down into the rain-soaked soil by the recoil of nearly continuous firing" only during lulls in combat.[24] In addition, German tank commander Otto Carius noted that Soviet soldiers used corduroy stands to prevent their artillery pieces and mortars from burrowing into the mud.[25]

Sledge explained the difficulty his crew had firing a mortar in mud. In early May 1945, his gunner had trouble maintaining the mortar's proper alignment and after firing several rounds the mortar crew moved the weapon for better footing. As the battle and the rain continued, the surface grew muddier, and recoil drove the base plate into the mud. Sledge reported that as they continued dropping rounds down the tube, his "mortar's base plate [drove] the pieces of wood supporting it deep into the mud in the bottom of the gun pit." Sledge's crew, without the wood supporting the weapon, could no longer be sure of the weapon's alignment and, subsequently, where any rounds might land. The mortar had to remain in its emplacement for the crew to operate it without being shot. Sledge and his comrades resolved the situation by retrieving helmetfuls of coral gravel, placing it in a deep hole, and lining the hole with boards. Sledge's crew also used box remnants to keep their rounds out of the mud.[26]

Wooden platforms are also essential for artillery. The weight of cannons and their recoil affects the efficient firing of artillery in mud. This was not true for early cannons and howitzers because they required crews to physically haul the weapon into position after each firing anyway. However, mud became more of an irritant when artillery developed more complex recoil systems that were meant to allow the weapon to shoot repeatedly at the same target. During the Falklands War in 1982, British gunners firing at Goose Green discovered while keeping their guns in action that the mud allowed "the trails to bury themselves almost to the layers' seats."[27]

When mud is present, engineers are essential. Like mechanics, military engineers are always in demand, so it should not be too shocking to note that commanders operating in muddy environments frequently ask for more engineers.

Even after combat operations the demand for more engineers to struggle with the mud is apparent. The Ninety-sixth Infantry Division, after fighting in the Philippines, stated that its one organic engineer battalion was "entirely inadequate in strength and equipment to support the Division." To hammer the point home, the division's "Action Against Enemy Report" concluded that the jungle and muddy conditions on Leyte "did more to slow down the advance of the [Ninety-sixth Infantry] Division in the later stages of the campaign than any action imposed by the enemy." The report recommended that adding just one combat engineer battalion "would have materially increased the combat effectiveness of this division."[28]

Providing a solution, the report's authors believed that one engineer battalion was insufficient and that each combat team needed its own engineer battalion in direct support. The American plan for the invasion of Okinawa estimated correctly that additional engineer equipment was essential. In fact, the Ninety-sixth Infantry Division's terrain and intelligence studies foresaw that road construction would be a major concern; therefore, engineer heavy equipment entered the battle for Okinawa well in excess of authorized levels but still proved inadequate.

They had learned from experiences with the Philippines monsoon but did not realize the power of Okinawa's rainy season.[29]

When too few trained engineers are available, other personnel are sometimes drafted as a labor source to combat the mud. The Thirty-fourth Infantry Division, after fighting in Italian mud, noted in its unit history that it had formed an ad hoc engineer unit from division personnel and attached units. These amateur engineers dug, added gravel, and drained excess water from disintegrating roads. Additionally, the conditions on Okinawa proved so impassable by June 1945 that truck drivers and their passengers hauled rubble by hand to spots in the road where the mud was at its worst.[30]

Large quantities of mud often compel engineers to provide materials continuously to maintain unsurfaced roads. In its area of operations, the Thirty-fourth Infantry Division placed 1,200 tons of rock in boggy areas even as

Combat engineers construct a corduroy road through the Hürtgen Forest in November 1944. *U.S. Army Military History Institute*

essential traffic continued to move.[31] In the Philippines, the 321st Engineer Battalion noted in a report that one road was in extremely bad condition despite receiving fifty loads of rock.[32] Although adding material was essential for road maintenance, situations did occur where trucks were required to stay off a road because using it caused faster damage than effort and materials could be extended to maintain it. Such a situation befell the 321st Engineer Battalion on Okinawa. A radio message from the battalion's commander to the 1140 Engineer Group requested that the Fiftieth Engineers not haul road-improvement materials using their Main Supply Route (MSR) despite the need for the gravel to keep roads in operation. The 1140 Engineer Group denied the request stating that the rain might not abate any time soon and that it was essential for the Fiftieth Engineers to haul the material necessary for maintaining the roads.[33]

CHAPTER 6

Mud and Morale

"I do not think it is too arbitrary to assert that in all the history of war, cold and snow have inflicted less misery and hardship on the soldier than has mud."[1]

—E. L. M. Burns

It is raining again. Mud!"[2] So wrote 2nd Lt. Don Jacques from Khe Sanh around October 1967 hinting about his situation. Combatants and historians know that mud hinders mobility. However, mud also has a drastic influence on morale, it is an uncomfortable part of daily life, and it exacerbates the weariness already inherent in war. Individuals who have spent most of their lives in the military, yet have never fired a shot in anger, know the trials that only wet soil can bring. Maj. Gen. F. M. Richardson wrote in *Fighting Spirit: A Study of Psychological Factors in War* that among the factors affecting morale were good health, good food, rest, and amenities such as books and clean, dry clothing.[3]

The effect of mud most remembered by soldiers overall—the soldier's general comfort—has had little influence on an operation's eventual outcome. The types of mud do not matter. Mud is mud to the soldier, and it is annoying. Richardson stated that clean, dry clothing is an important element of morale, and George Orwell addressed this quite well: "War is, quite literally, a dirty business. Living in the field, in a trench, under a poncho or in the shelter of a ruined building, makes men dirty in a way that almost beggars description."[4]

Mud not only prevents a soldier from having clean, dry clothing but also affects his or her physical appearance and adds to the individual's general discomfort. Although the misery of fighting and dying in the mud can contribute to a decline in morale, mud alone rarely —if ever—diminishes morale to the point of mission failure. However, numerous examples exist of soldiers' feelings of irritation and frustration brought on by mud. For example, during and after General Burnside's Mud March, desertion increased, and mud's effect was a major reason.[5] Bill Mauldin, trying to convey the experience of American infantrymen, proposed that noncombatants back in the United States "dig a hole in your back yard while it is raining. Sit in the hole until the water climbs up around your ankles. Pour cold mud down your shirt collar. Sit there for forty-eight hours."[6] While on Peleliu, E. B. Sledge explained that after boot camp's heavy indoctrination concerning personal and equipment cleanliness, it was difficult for him to tolerate being dirty. He was not the only marine to feel that way, even though staying clean in combat was nearly impossible. He added, "It has always puzzled me that this important factor in our daily lives has received so little attention from historians and often is omitted from otherwise excellent personal memoirs by infantrymen."[7] Crusting to one's uniform and skin, dry caked-on mud was simply irritating. Recalling an instance on World War I's Western Front, Lieutenant Rommel wrote, "Our clothes were crusted over with a thick coat of dried mud and this together with our lowered physical condition, made marching very hard."[8] Many soldiers had a terrible disdain for the feeling of mud crusted to their skin; and, for the most part, they ignored it, but it was always there.

Mud causes clothing to deteriorate. Soil and excessive water combined with the wear and tear that infantrymen endure wreaks havoc on uniforms. World War I's muddy trenches forced Highland regiments of the British Army to develop protective shields for their kilts. The mud was so deep and pervasive that expensive tartans lost their distinctive coloring and the material frayed. Gottlob Bidermann, fighting in the Crimea against Soviet troops, remembered envying soldiers outfitted with new clothing and gear, while he and his comrades "struggled through the mud in uniforms and equipment that were tattered, encrusted and faded."[9] Maj. Paul Grauwin recollected that at Dien Bien Phu the temperatures were warm enough to allow the defenders to roll their pants to the knees. In this way, they could save their trousers and reduce any additional mud they might carry in their trouser legs.[10]

Well-trained soldiers have a strong inclination to keep their equipment clean. Even when covered in mud, the indoctrination and commonsense attitude toward a weapon's cleanliness can pervade lulls in combat. When time is available, or a move to a rear area is apparent, veterans have often taken any spare time to bathe or shower, shave, and scrape mud from their clothes.[11] Usually, soldiers used their hands to remove the mud, but heavily caked-on mud needed a tool. German infantryman Harry Mielert wrote that he and his comrades removed mud from their German army uniforms "first with knives, then with wire brushes and last through washing."[12] In some situations, however, emphasis on cleanliness seemed ridiculous. Spc. 4 Matt Jones found an order to have highly shined boots during Vietnam's monsoon season ludicrous. As part of the First Cavalry

Division, shined boots were the order of the day, but after returning from field operations, his boots were covered in mud. Digging and scraping at the mud with a knife helped, but even wearing his boots in the shower did not remove all the mud. Jones recalled more than one occasion when he polished right over the mud "so that it would look like part of the boot, and eventually it just became part of the boot."[13]

Removing mud and dirt from clothing helps maintain the uniform and improves the hygiene of soldiers; but deleting mud from weapons is more practical.[14] In April 1917, British infantryman George Bloomfield was cleaning his rifle. As it slipped, he tried to grab it and prevent it from "falling into the mud," but the weapon discharged and killed another soldier.[15] Sledge also recalled a filthy marine who endeavored to keep his light machine gun relatively clean by setting "the handle on his toe to keep it off the mud."[16]

Although commanders know the health benefits of cleanliness and believe in the improvement in morale that follows, many times the act of bathing seems pointless. Guy Sajer noted that because of the slick muddy conditions surrounding field shower points in World War II, "those who got through the showers first often found themselves tossed onto their backsides in the liquid mud which flooded the outskirts of the camp."[17] As American officers in the European Theater of Operations Lt. Harold Leinbaugh and Lt. John Campbell wrote, "twenty days in muddy holes left them unshaven, fatigued, and in need of showers and clean clothing more than anything on earth."[18] During the Kosovo intervention, Sgt. Charlotte Russell decided that if given a choice between negotiating the gravel pathways in her morass of a camp and clambering over the rocks alongside them, she and her fellow soldiers preferred the rocks "because by the time you get back from a bath you're smashed again with mud."[19]

The acceptance of mud on the body and a willingness to become dirty often marks the veteran soldier from the inexperienced one because modern military establishments emphasize cleanliness to new recruits. This attitude is difficult to shrug off even during initial encounters with hostile fire and sometimes combatants' reluctance to immerse themselves in mud proved fatal. However, if they survived their first battle, inexperienced soldiers learned a valuable lesson. In Italy during World War II, incoming artillery forced a British wireman, but not the three American artillerymen who were with him, to dive into a ditch full of soft mud. When the excitement was over the Americans asked the British wireman why he jumped into the mud. The soldier retorted, "A body can always wipe the mud off, not so easy to wipe iron out."[20] In November 1944, Sgt. Allen Towne noticed that "at first, a new man would be reluctant to drop to the cold wet ground when a shell came over, especially if his clothes were dry, and he was not used to crawling in the mud."[21]

A muddy, weary, and hungry PFC Jerry W. Standridge after two solid days of combat in Long An Province, Vietnam. *U.S. Military History Institute*

Conversely, mud, when covering a soldier, can imply combat experience whether he or she deserves the status or not. Mud on a combatant's uniform gives inexperienced soldiers the impression that they are in the presence of an experienced fighter. The idea is similar to high school football players who participate in the game and thus on their uniforms have mud or grass stains that separates them from those in pristine uniforms who did not play. Hence, mud becomes part of a combatant's everyday life, and some even feel that they are not veterans until they are in the mud. Wilfred Owen, writing to his mother in January 1917, told her that he was "let down, gently, into the real thing, Mud," which had worked its way into his sleeping bag and pajamas. He added, "For I sleep on a stone floor and the servant squashed mud on all my belongings; I suppose by way of baptism."[22] As Napoleon retreated in 1814, Old Guard veterans initially teased young conscripts, but after the newcomers faced Russian veterans, the Old Guard cheered their return from battle, "covered with mud and blood," which changed their status from unproven draftees to veteran troops. Although exposure to mud during initial training did not make German tank driver Henry Metelmann a veteran, the mud proved to be the common element between the heroes of Verdun, the Somme, Flanders, and Tannenberg and his becoming a soldier. "Mud was no mere common substance any more, it was the element in which our heroes had died valiantly at Passchendaele."[23]

Age and prior military experience were also factors in mud's influences on morale. Two veterans of World War I commented on what kind of soldier best endured the trenches. Siegfried Sassoon, a British officer in World War II, believed that teenagers had the most difficult time: "mud and boredom and discomfort seemed to take all the guts out of them."[24]

Lord Moran stated that winter in Flanders's mud affected men differently and that regular soldiers proved most adaptable, as they had spent many years under spartan conditions. Short service volunteers, however, did not withstand the privations as well.[25] Historian Dennis Showalter noted a similar attitude when soldiers referred to experienced leaders in muddy terms, thus acknowledging combat experience and possibly a competent superior. Showalter wrote that General Paulus, although a good staff officer, was a "soft-shoe-type rather than a muddy-boots commander."[26]

Spending a long time in any type of mud, especially Type I, is just one of several means by which mud can lower fighting spirit. Even seasonal mud tends to lower morale, as do those times when the soil's soft condition hampers mission progress. Long static periods in constant contact with mud also wear down morale. In addition, a good way to judge combatants' feelings about mud is to examine the relief they feel when lifted from it.

Seasonal mud is horrible for those combatants forced to fight in it. Admittedly, the dreary skies and rain are a significant reason for poor morale, but mud is a major contributor to a combatant's depressed spirit. For example, a British veteran of Burma recalling the monsoon for the television series *The World at War* proclaimed that "squashing through mud, living in mud, lying in mud, and sleeping in mud, and drinking in mud, and eating in mud. That was the monsoon in Burma; it's just a nightmare."[27]

Additionally, one historian noted that a difficult march through rain and mud caused a loss of morale among Indian soldiers maneuvering to fend off a Japanese attack in Burma.[28] The morale-eroding seasonal mud changed very little from Burma to Okinawa. Sledge remembered it this way:

This was my first taste of mud in combat, and it was more detestable than I had ever imagined. Mud in camp on Pavuvu was a nuisance. Mud on maneuvers was an inconvenience. But mud on the battlefield was misery beyond description. I had seen photographs of World War I troops in the mud—the men grinning, of course, if the picture was posed. If not posed, the faces always wore a peculiarly forlorn, disgusted expression, an expression I now understand.[29]

Spc. 4 Jones remembered that in Vietnam the "monsoon was a downer, everybody was pissed." He also recalled that when the monsoon came "mud was everywhere" and caked onto everything including boots, which might have a few pounds of mud attached to them.[30]

Spending more than a day or two in the soul-sapping qualities of mud causes poor morale. The area around Manassas in February 1862 was "the *rainiest— snowiest—muddiest* and with all, the most disagreeable country I ever met up with" according to Confederate officer James Griffin. Later, after trying to build some new batteries for two weeks, he added, "I never was so heartily tired of mud and water in my life."[31] Near Marietta, Georgia, in June 1864, General Williams noted that after three days of heavy storms "the earth became saturated like a soaked sponge and the mud was intolerable." His despair deepened as he postulated that "the mud seemed too deep to ever dry up."[32] The importance of lengthy durations in the mud is apparent in two letters written by an Indian veterinarian in British service. In September 1916, he explained his suffering in the frequent rain and mud but pointed out that he had grown accustomed to the inconvenience. However, seven months later, he continued to complain about the conditions in France stating that mud was splattered up to the necks of the horses and that he could not understand how life could continue under such environmental conditions.[33] Some combatants referred to their mud experiences in surreal terms. Sledge wrote that heavy rains, which lasted for two days straight in early May 1945, were a foreshadowing of the hellish mud he would suffer in for a minimum of two weeks.[34] A month of snow was just as intolerable when it finally melted. In Italy, it snowed nearly every day during February 1944 leaving the troops with a "depressing struggle against mud. . . giving all ranks more to worry about than the enemy."[35]

Relating closely to long periods of direct contact with mud are long periods in the same location. Although certain situations forced static warfare, such as the trenches of World War I, camps where soldiers sat and waited for the next mission also fostered the physical and emotional toll from mud. Siegfried Sassoon wrote that "the main characteristics of Camp 13 were mud and smoke. Mud was everywhere." He added that a wet day caused some grumbling and reduced the camp at Heilly "to its natural condition—a swamp."[36] In late November 1917, British stretcher bearer Dunham found a similar situation in his camp at Simencourt. The location was a sea of ankle-deep mud, nothing existed to help them pass the time, and "no-one fancied strolling out in the mud."[37] During the Battle of Dutch Harbor, the bivouac areas swelled "with mud and oozing tundra," and long periods in a muddy camp taxed the morale of soldiers so much that one of them, Lucian Wernick, recalled how an encounter with a valley of wildflowers altered his mood. "The contrast between that and the total muddy drabness of our base made a poet out of this completely non-poetic soul."[38]

In some instances, the muddy conditions became an annoyance of such magnitude that combatants risked their lives to avoid it. Recalling his experiences as a junior officer, the future Field Marshal Lord Wavell related one particular World War I trench inspection. "I once found the whole garrison of a trench sitting on the parapet, preferring the risk of enemy bullets to the mud in the trench."[39] Wilfred Owen also reached his fill of saturated soil and took his chances above the trenches rather than deal with the mud. "I went up to the front in the usual way–or nearly the usual way, for I felt too weak to wrestle with the mud, and sneaked along the top."[40]

Mud often provides a better image of war's reality than innocent thoughts of glory and medals. Young men raised on tales of heroic last stands and dashing cavalry charges see war's true face when mud, among many other factors, destroys their youthful dreams. The mud almost overwhelmed Sledge in 1945. His memories of the mud, desolation, and utter disgust survive in his memoirs written more than thirty years later. Sledge recalled that the area around his foxhole on Half Moon Hill was a horrible-smelling dung heap replete with mud, decaying corpses, maggots, and the debris of battle. "If a marine slipped and slid down the back slope of the muddy ridge, he was apt to reach the bottom vomiting."[41]

Lack of mission progress especially that caused by mud, lowered combatants' morale. Whether the task was completing an offensive objective, building an airstrip, or constructing a road, the presence of large quantities of mud often made mission accomplishment more difficult. During the War of 1812's New Orleans campaign, British soldiers received orders to retrieve two large cannons from their exposed positions. However, a tactical setback combined with rain and mud had destroyed their morale. Rather than drag the valuable guns through a plain of mud, the men "abandoned the task and stole away in the darkness."[42] The Flanders offensive launched in late July 1918 and continuing into the wettest August in four years took a toll. According to the future Lieutenant General Burns, "the first four weeks of the offensive had cost 68,000 British casualties, and the strain of fighting in the mud and the lack of real success in the attacks had begun to tell on morale."[43] Diminished morale was a problem for one engineer company in Vietnam when mud slowed the progress of its mission. On the one hand, according to Lamar Myers, "you get tired of ankle- to knee-deep mud, walking in it, working in it, trying to put culverts into it, trying to get it cleared out."[44] On the other hand, as conditions improved and mud began to dry, morale rose among soldiers who saw progress in their efforts. Such was the case for airfield engineers in February 1943. After six days of Pacific rain and its subsequent mud, weather conditions improved, and the unit added a half foot of material to the runway, improving the men's morale as their unit moved toward mission accomplishment.[45]

A close association can develop between the infantry and the mud. Support troops who are outside of the plight of the muddy battlefields often sympathize with those combatants that World War I British soldiers referred to as the Poor Bloody Infantry. In veterans' recollections, mud figures prominently in the trenches. Burns expressed this well when he wrote how soldiers who did not serve on the front lines "felt a certain humility when they compared their lot with that of the infantryman."[46] German tank gunner Karl Fuchs, writing a letter home to his wife during World War II, admitted that he had little reason to complain when he pondered the life of other German soldiers "stuck in the mud, water, and terrible conditions."[47] Likewise, a staff officer fighting the Japanese at Kohima during the monsoon stated "the infantry, as usual, get the worst of it."[48]

One way of telling how miserable mud makes combatants is to understand the joy they feel when they leave it. Before the 1806 Battle of Pultusk, French soldiers moved out of their bivouac site with enthusiasm, as they wished to put the mud behind them.[49] Frank Dunham recalled how better weather made him feel in February 1918. "The sunshine was glorious, and it soon dried the mud, for which we were thankful."[50] Not surprisingly, E. B. Sledge also preferred days with beautiful skies. In early June 1945, he enjoyed picking up ammunition, rations, and other necessities, despite the labor of "running through the mud." However, Sledge hated cloudy days, partly for the potential of more rain, but more important because it prevented American aircraft from flying and dropping supplies by air. The result was that the essential material had to be hauled across the quagmire.[51]

However, German soldiers on World War II's Eastern Front did not always appreciate the sun and clear skies, even if they did dry the mud. Unlike Sledge, Sajer preferred the dark skies, rain, and subsequent mud. "Despite our heavy, waterlogged clothes, wornout boots, fever, and the impossibility of lying down except on the soaking ground, we blessed fortune for sending us gray skies and rain," adding that all the negative aspects of weather to infantrymen, wind, rain, and lots of thick clouds, were better than "clear skies, which invariably meant the humming planes."[52]

Having survived some greater challenge, some veterans could discount the annoyance of mud. Being in or out of the mud mattered little to Sajer when his life was at risk. He and his fellow soldiers, after having crossed the Dnieper River in 1943, "stepped, one after the other, onto the solid earth—which is to say, onto a quagmire exactly like the east bank. But the mud no longer mattered; we had crossed to the other side."[53] Similarly, Pvt. Abe Yoshizo remarked that in Burma he and his comrades "were all dirty like mud dolls, but everyone was so happy that we had passed through the critical line safely, undetected by the enemy."[54]

More often than not, mud is one of many environmental factors responsible for a decline in morale. William Manchester claimed that Australians on New Guinea "joked about the five M's—mosquitoes, mud, mountains, malaria, and monotony."[55] Trying to build a helicopter base in Kosovo, American soldiers faced the potential morale breaker of mud in what one twenty-year veteran, CWO Gregory Schneider, called "the muddiest" location he knew. The executive officer of the U.S. Army's Twelfth Aviation Brigade, Lt. Col. Mike Dixon, recognized that 3 inches of rain and marble-sized hail made living conditions difficult and thus it became essential in such a location to "keep up the morale."[56]

One of the more common elements associated closely with mud and a poor attitude is cold rain. Mud has no constant temperature but fluctuates according to the air that surrounds it or the liquid that comprises it. Unless warm mud is at or near the boiling point, such as that found in mud pots found in volcanic regions (an uncommon occurrence), then it seldom affects soldiers adversely. However, cold mud does affect a soldier's morale and health. Mud and the human body most often intersect at the feet, and since most soldiers wear boots, few veterans mention marching specifically in cold mud.

However, during the Italian campaign, members of the U.S. Army's 631st Field Artillery Battalion hated that their German foe was warm and dry in houses while they suffered in the "cold rain and mud." American artillery fire "on a house filled with 'Krauts' usually brought them tumbling out of windows and doors to water-filled fox-holes and mud-lined caves,"[57] allowing the Germans to share in the battalion's misery. Also operating in Italy, the Thirty-fourth Infantry Division reported in December 1944 that "high winds, rain and mud were supplemented by heavy snows. . . . The weather gradually became colder, making life for front line troops that much more miserable."[58] American infantryman George Lucht, fighting in Germany during World War II, decided to wear his heavy overcoat rather than his field jacket. Regrettably, this large coat acted like a sponge in the rain and added more weight to his body. Recalling a firefight, Lucht recounted that "we were hit by heavy fire, and I was half mud, half water. The cold was terrible. I'll tell you the truth, I felt like giving up the struggle."[59]

Having to fight in mud's miserable and loathsome character is not impossible, and one reason mud receives such little attention is that unlike bombs, bullets, bayonets, and environmental factors such as cold, heat, and water, mud can drown a soldier but otherwise does not kill directly. Yet few things are as ignoble to combatants as dying in the mud.

Soldiers face death—it is the nature of war—but dying in the mud correlates to a loss of human dignity. The horrors of the Passchendaele battlefield were so demoralizing that Bombadier J. W. Palmer recalled that witnessing men "dying in the slime. . . absolutely finished me off."[60] Henry Metelmann recalled the retaliation killing of a Russian prisoner for shooting a German general at point-blank range. German soldiers beat him to death with rifle butts, "slain like a rat into the mud."[61] Veterans, in order to preserve some sense of dignity to the dead, hated leaving a friend's body in the mud, especially face down. On Okinawa, Lt. Reginald Fincke witnessed "two men trying to hold a bloated corpse out of the mud." When asked why they did it, one of the men replied that they just wanted "to get him to a safe and dry place."[62]

Mud hides dead bodies. Walking through a trench knee deep in Type IIa mud, Burns remembered stepping on something soft, "the rear end of a dead German." The dead soldier, "visible in places through the mud, was green. By that time we had been living for many days in the stink and visible presence of dead men, and this very horrid sight excited no more than a moment's shock and disgust."[63] On Okinawa, marines could only shovel mud over dead Japanese corpses in front of their positions, and Sledge witnessed how explosions kept uncovering them.[64] Grauwin noted, as the Battle of Dien Bien Phu ended, that the dead "sank into the mud, and those who came in from the support posts walked over them, and they sank in a little deeper." The relentless, draining aspect of mud follows soldiers even to their deaths.[65]

Although mud carries numerous bacteria, some combatants have used mud's insular effect in a beneficial manner. Mud can trap heat and, when combined with natural body oils, can provide protection against the cold. According to John Keegan's *The Face of Battle*, on the night before Waterloo, "Simmons, a lieutenant of the 1st/95th Rifles, smeared an old blanket with thick clayey mud and lay down under it on some straw. He kept quite warm."[66] Wilfred Owen stated that a half blanket spread on him as he lay in the mud provided as much perceived warmth as "the rising of the May-day sun" and that his experiences on the Somme in 1917 were such "that nothing daunts me now."[67] During World War II, one American soldier learned that, "in welcoming his first shower in two months, he was also washing away the layer of grime and body grease that, however unaesthetic, protected him against the European cold."[68]

Occasionally, soldiers actually enjoyed the mud. Mud provided some soldiers, because of youth or an upperclass upbringing, either amusement or at least a change of pace. In World War I, Gen. Sir Wilmot

Herringham's enlisted nephew seemed "cheerful . . . dripping wet with water and mud" and told his uncle that not having bathed or removed his clothes for two days was "a novelty."[69] Many Americans presently seek opportunities to drive off-road vehicles over muddy tracks while others enjoy a game of mud volleyball and other similar pursuits. While serving in Vietnam, Matt Jones enjoyed racing motorized cargo carriers and playing football and baseball in the mud.[70] However, others thought much differently about such muddy attempts at recreation. Commanders believed that one of the best ways to raise morale was through organized sports, but Brian Garfield noted that with strong winds and lots of mud, "baseball games only added to frustration."[71]

CHAPTER 7

Mud and Health

"At night, crouching in a shell-hole and filling it, the mud watches, like an enormous octopus. The victim arrives. It throws its poisonous slobber out at him, blinds him, closes round him, buries him. . . . For men die of mud as they die of bullets, but more horribly. Mud is where men sink and—what is worse—where there soul sinks. . . Hell is not fire, that would not be the ultimate in suffering. Hell is mud!"[1]
—*Martin Gilbert*

In late October 1914, advancing German forces found themselves in "a liquid trap which yawned to engulf them. Beneath the muddy waters were hidden ditches and canals into which men would suddenly plunge over their heads, and bottomless mud which would hold them fast in the flood." So wrote historian Douglas Johnson about World War I's Battle of the Yser when the Western powers opened the sleuces and let in sea water.[2]

Mud debilitates soldiers. It causes illness and death. Notorious accounts of individuals and animals sinking to their deaths in large mud holes exist, and although few ever strike a note of credibility, some accounts are authentic. The following examples come from primary sources who either witnessed a drowning or knew the conditions that allowed drowning in mud.

Some of the more convincing instances concern mules. During the American Civil War, Gen. Alpheus Williams wrote that mules drowned more than once. On January 24, 1863, he told his daughter in a letter "one could not go a mile without drowning mules in mud-holes. It is solemnly true that we lost mules in the middle of the road, sinking out of sight in the mud-holes. A few bubbles of air, a stirring of the watery mud, indicated the last expiring efforts of many a poor long-ears." On another occasion, mud indirectly caused mules to drown. In late May 1862, General Williams's command forded the Potomac River where it was 300 feet wide and fast moving. As his wagons descended into the river, they became stuck on the muddy bank and the swift current prevented men from rescuing the stranded mules, which were hitched to the wagons and unable to move. Subsequently, the mules drowned.[3]

Combatants drown in mud. More often than not, the victims are wounded soldiers unable to "swim" out of copious amounts of mud or too weak to fight its suctioning effect. Although drowning was not the cause of death for the following statistic, sinking in deep mud might explain why the British could not account for more than fifty thousand British and Commonwealth soldiers who fought in Flanders.[4] Type I mud's inability to support large amounts of weight means that combatants can drown in mud when wounded, when weighed down with excessive amounts of equipment, or simply because the mud is too deep. At New Orleans in 1815, Lt. George Gleig recounted the mud drowning of a soldier as the British retreated through a swamp. Gleig, hearing the stricken soldier call for help, attempted to pull the man from chest-deep mud. Despite his effort, the soldier sank from view, and Gleig found himself up to his armpits with nothing solid beneath him. He too cried for help and was dragged to safety with the aid of a leather canteen strap, "but the poor soldier had been swallowed by the swamp."[5] At Passchendaele, Pvt. Cyril Lee recalled how he and some other soldiers tried to save a wounded soldier struggling in Type I mud. "The look on the lad's face, it was really pathetic. . . . But I couldn't do a thing, had I bent a little more I should have gone in with him. Had anyone gone near this sea of mud we should have gone in with him as so many did."[6] Sgt. William Manchester, a Marine veteran of World War II's Pacific Theater, related how mud caused a death on Okinawa: "One night Wally Moon was buried alive, suffocated in his one-man foxhole—he always insisted on sleeping alone—by sheets of mud from exploding shells."[7] PFC John Dabonka of the U.S. Army's Sixtieth Infantry Regiment stated in March 1967, "Two men from my company drowned. They got stuck in the mud and couldn't get out because of all the equipment they had on. What a way to go."[8]

As mud can kill by drowning, it also can kill combatants indirectly when it acts as a vector for such bacteria as tetanus and anthrax, which live in the soil. For combatants and animals, skin is the best barrier to germs and disease, but one result of war is that skin tends to tear, scratch, and burn. As long as "dirt does not enter into the wound . . . the patient's chances of survival are better."[9] Hence, mud with its plasticity is an efficient agent in spreading bacteria.

Soldiers have always had a close connection with dirt, but sieges are one of the few battle modes in which combatants purposefully dig into the earth. After the Industrial Revolution, warfare became more efficient,

more deadly, and from the Crimean War to the present
the digging of trenches and other fortifications increased.
Linear warfare disappeared when weapons became more
efficient, and soldiers deliberately hugged the earth, increasing their contact with soil-based organisms. World
War I's trenches and all the chaos caused by more efficient weapons created new difficulties for medical science. The powerful weapons of World War I "caused
deep, jagged wounds, nearly all of which were contami-
nated with tetanus and gas gangrene."[10]

To further emphasize the significance of soil bacteria, an American surgical manual written in 1943 stated
that injuries that broke the skin introduced mud and other
material from the battlefield superficially or deep into
the wound. "In a bacteriological study of 317 fresh war
wounds," 93 percent had at least one species of bacteria
and nearly three quarters of these wounds had two or
more species.[11] Marines on Guadalcanal knew that soils
were unsanitary, so several men lifted Lt. Col. Lewis B.
(Chesty) Puller onto a poncho "to get him off the ground
and avoid tetanus infection" when he suffered a wound.[12]
Deep mud pulling at boots too big for his feet caused
German machine gunner Günter Koschorrek to consider
throwing them away and going barefoot. He decided to
keep the ill-fitting boots, however, when he considered
the "infections and other problems" that barefoot soldiers had "picked up from the mud."[13] During a lengthy
diatribe on Dien Bien Phu's mud, Paul Grauwin wrote,
"Soil infections, always a great anxiety to military sur-
geons, became disastrous. Every shell splinter took mud
into the body with it." As he probed his patients' injuries, he found mud beyond the initial wound and deep
in the muscle fibers.[14]

World War I highlighted another hazard found in
mud: gas gangrene, a condition that has nothing to do
with poison gas attacks and "is an entity in itself, differ-

ent from other kinds of gangrene."[15] Gas gangrene developed from the heavily cultivated soils of France and
Flanders, which contained a bacillus originating from
horse manure. The bacillus found its way onto soldiers'
uniforms, and when struck by a bullet or shrapnel, made
its way into the body through the impregnated uniform.[16]

However, bacteria do not require deep jagged
wounds for access into the body. With Type IIa mud's
liquid quality as a means, even scratches provide easy
entry for dangerous infections. Mud was a huge problem for Grauwin. When asked about a patient's status
he reported, "Tetanus, sir. He has no wound. I can
only suppose that the mud must have infected a scratch
in his leg." Aware of the increased risk his charges
faced fighting in large quantities of mud, Grauwin
gave injections of penicillin and streptomycin because
infections could move quickly when mud infiltrated
a wound. When the temperature on one of his patients

Troops of the Ninth Infantry Division take soggy positions
in a Vietnam rice paddy in 1967. *U.S. Army Military
History Institute*

rose suddenly after treatment, Grauwin knew that mud had infiltrated the wound despite the dressing and caused infection.[17]

With all the bacteria that hides in mud, it is in a combatant's best interest to stay as clean as possible, which, of course, is one reason military training includes such an emphasis on staying clean. During the age of linear warfare when soldiers stood to fight, many may have maintained some semblance of cleanliness. However, the nature of more recent conflicts requires veterans to lie, crawl, and dig in the soil. They become muddy.

The first action many soldiers undertake when returning from the field is to bathe, as did Spc. 4 Michael Romano in 1969 in Vietnam. "I never saw so much mud in all my life. I was covered with it. We got back about an hour ago, and I took a bath in the river."[18] Matt Jones found an easier way to wash away the mud. Most, if not all, American maintenance shops in Vietnam had hoses, which were very convenient for removing mud from one's boots. As a helicopter crewman, Jones had access to a maintenance shop and used its hose to clean his helicopter's interior, soiled by infantrymen passengers who pounded the mud from their boots during their rides in his Huey. The hose also removed the mud that dried on the bottom of the helicopter as the rotor wash always pasted mud on its underside whenever it arrived and departed from a muddy landing zone.[19]

Hygiene is especially crucial in and around medical facilities. Although efforts to sanitize an area in a war zone are often self-defeating, medical units try their best, and when mud is present, this task becomes even more difficult. One reason for medical facilities' unsanitary conditions is that combatants rarely, if ever, reach an aid station or hospital clean. Siegfried Sassoon, when he was wounded, noted that "many of us still had the caked mud of the war zone on our boots and clothes, and every bandaged man was accompanied by his battle experience."[20] A doctor on Guadalcanal, working on the chest of a Marine casualty, wore only one shoe in 6 to 8 inches of mud, "the last hope of sanitation gone."[21] Deteriorating sanitary conditions were what Major Grauwin recollected in April 1954, "Blood, vomit, and feces mixed with the mud made up a frightful compound."[22]

The officer in charge of trying to find a site on which to establish a military aid station or field hospital will choose the cleanest, most sanitary spot possible. During the Battle of the Bulge, Capt. George Lytton was a battalion surgeon. When interviewed about his experience in mud, he replied that he always chose sites on paved roads where mud was less of a factor, thus increasing its sanitary conditions.[23] However, medical bunkers, necessary in many circumstances, were often unsanitary. The mud became such a problem for French medical personnel at Dien Bien Phu that they resorted to extreme measures to maintain sanitary conditions. Heavy artillery bombardment from the Viet Minh necessitated Major Grauwin's use of a muddy bunker despite the poor sanitary conditions. When the monsoon arrived, the moisture seeped through the bunker's earthen roof long after the rain fell, and finally "the time came when the earth floor could absorb no more and was covered with a soft, slippery mud." Grauwin found it very difficult to maneuver in his hospital because of the mud's suctioning effect, but he feared going barefoot because concealed in the mud were "broken needles and glass which cut the soles of the feet." By May 1954, the mud had risen to knee level. As a result, some wounded soldiers hung in stretchers from the medical bunker's roof to keep themselves out of the mud. The medical personnel also slept suspended from the ceiling and by morning, their clothes were dry, but they still lowered themselves down into the mud for another day. In addition, water was scarce, and Grauwin knew that more water was necessary to clean the wounded. "Around me I could see nothing but mud, mud everywhere, on the ground, on the beds, on clothes and dressings, on tables, in wounds, and on faces and hands." More than once, he saw the bare legs of men covered in mud and would sometimes notice that "under this sheath of mud, there was the thickness made by a field dressing."

Even after he performed operations that saved legionnaires' lives, the conditions in which they recovered were deplorable. As the siege worsened, the small hospital bunker was the only place for serious casualties and the wounded had no place to rest. Those waiting for aid remained "outside, in the rain, under fire, in the mud." Major Grauwin, his bunker filled to capacity, recalled how the wounded "squatted there in the mud. They had to be washed, and their dressings, which were

"Goo-shoo" coverings on the left, standard boots on the right, with the former advantages apparent. Capua sector, Italy, November 1943. *National Archives*

befouled through and through had to be changed." However, clean bandages became scarcer as the wounded increased and as the French lost more and more of their defensive position to the Viet Minh.[24]

Some medical units found a better way to stay out of the mud and maintain some semblance of sanitary conditions. One method was to use amphibious tractors for mobile aid stations. Such a station could turn aside most small arms rounds, and the First Marine Division on Okinawa found that "during heavy rain and deep mud it afforded a dry, protected operating room." These makeshift aid stations also provided medical personnel with a clean working environment rather than "standing in mud and water up to their ankles."[25]

Sgt. William Manchester wrote that Type I and IIa mud made it difficult to use a rifle and bayonet as a post for hanging plasma bottles. "The gruel of Okinawa mud was so thin that it couldn't support a rifle bayonet; men had to be withdrawn from the line to hold the containers."[26] In addition, Type IIa mud, with its high moisture content, conveyed electricity. A few welders working in World War II's Pacific Theater suffered severe shocks when they worked in deep mud to repair vehicles.[27]

Despite its many negative health influences, mud has some positive medicinal value. An old folk remedy for certain wounds was a poultice of mud and vegetation, and, in a pinch, an application of mud also served to discourage pests. According to *Honey, Mud, and Maggots*, "soldiers serving in tropical areas will cover their faces and hands with mud to protect themselves against mosquitoes and gnats, just as other animals will roll in mud holes or bogs."[28] During the Vietnam War, U.S. Navy diver Steven Waterman remembered the painful biting of red ants that had fallen down his shirt. Mud proved to be effective in keeping the insects at bay. "I cleared them off, buttoned my collar and sleeves, and packed handfuls of mud around my neck and wrists. Then I smeared the gray mud over all the exposed skin of my face and hands. In the heat, this poultice dried to a concrete-like consistency," and he had no further difficulties with ants.[29] Although it was unhygienic, some American veterans of World War I used mud for its moisture. Two hours of marching toward Belleau Wood without food or water induced some marines to drink water from wagon ruts when they found it, while others used "mud from the roads to moisten their tongues."[30]

Sieges and static warfare existed before the early twentieth century, but trenchfoot came to the world's attention during World War I. Although not a mortal injury, trenchfoot not only affects a soldier's health and morale, but it also debilitates unit readiness. Water and cold temperatures are trenchfoot's main ingredients, but the depth and fluid nature of Type I and IIa muds, respectively, also encourages the malady. Army medic Sgt. Allen Towne defined the ailment, now known as immersion foot, as "persistent dampness or immersion of the feet in water. It can result in permanent damage to the peripheral vessels of the lower limbs." Geographer John Collins stated that trenchfoot began "with numbness, followed by swelling, terrible pain and, in untreated cases, gangrene."[31] He added that during World War II "trench foot assumed epidemic proportions among U.S. combat infantrymen who for days on end waded rather than marched through chilly muck."[32] General Herringham recalled that during World War I it was difficult to rotate soldiers to and from the frontline trenches. He and other officers knew that reducing exposure in the muddy trenches was best to prevent this new malady, but in certain areas the German positions overlooked the British lines, which made relieving various units "so dangerous that it could not be carried out at short intervals."[33]

Medical officers tried various ways to prevent trenchfoot. The most obvious solution was to keep soldiers out of cold, wet mud. The monthly sanitation report for February 1945 provided by the U.S. Army's 133rd Infantry Regiment said the regiment tried to keep frontline soldiers dry by providing overhead cover for the positions, dug drainage ditches around them, and placed stones at the bottom of entrenchments to keep the soldiers from standing long hours in the mud.[34]

Trenchfoot had a tremendous influence on personnel strength. In March 1916, after four days in the Ypres sector, the Second Royal Scots evacuated a hundred soldiers or a quarter of its strength for exhaustion and trenchfoot, and by war's end 74,711 British soldiers were hospitalized for trenchfoot and frostbite.[35] One British medical officer recounted a foot inspection he conducted. After the men had "wiped off the damp mud with their socks . . . [I] pulled myself together and went and looked

Soldiers test mud shoes at Camp Gordon, Johnston, Florida, in January 1943. *National Archives*

at their feet, red, swollen and deformed beneath their coat of mud." He admitted to feeling guilt when he had to send these men back into the trenches.[36] During the Battle of the Bulge, U.S. Army doctor George Lytton estimated that as soon as the snow began to thaw the number of trenchfoot cases increased to 10 percent of his unit.[37] In late May 1945, the unit report for the U.S. Army's 381st Infantry Regiment estimated that combat efficiency for the unit was at 75 percent due to the duration and amount of rain resulting in more cases of trenchfoot.[38] By 1945, trenchfoot claimed nearly forty-five thousand U.S. infantrymen in the European Theater.[39]

Footwear can be a godsend or a curse, depending on the type of mud in which it is worn. In muds with high moisture content, good footwear is essential for preventing trenchfoot. However, boots and shoes with poor soles or shoddy construction allow combatants to slip, slide, and lose their boots in the mud.

Good footwear was the best method that General Herringham used for halting trenchfoot during World War I. He realized quite early that good boots were essential. To ameliorate trenchfoot, he first ordered soldiers to loosen their boots and puttees and issued them two pairs of socks and a "larger size of boot." These measures were helpful for cold temperatures, but not for wet feet, the condition most conducive to trenchfoot. Subsequently, soldiers had their feet "washed, dried, and greased" before moving up to the frontlines and then had the process repeated once a day. These procedures had some benefit, but Herringham knew that waterproof boots were necessary. The British army tried Japanese waterproof stockings made of paper, but they did not withstand the test of the trenches. They also tried Canadian lumber boots and Norwegian field boots, but they did not meet expectations either. What finally seemed to work were waterproof thigh boots, which arrived in the winter of 1915. However, these boots did not totally prevent moisture from reaching the feet, as mud was sometimes higher than the boot tops. Still, Herringham noted that, with the arrival of waterproof thigh boots and the improvement of trenches, he never saw as many affected feet as in 1915.[40] In late November 1916, Frank Dunham welcomed the issuance of rubber waders, as did all his fellow soldiers.[41] Wilfred Owen, writing home to his mother, mentioned that his rubber waders made him appear like a Cromwellian trooper and added, "The waders are of course indispensable. In two and a half miles of trench which I waded yesterday there was not one inch of dry ground."[42]

During World War II, the U.S. military tried other types of boots to keep feet dry. The War Department issued troops a type of boot called shoe pacs intended to reduce trenchfoot casualties induced by excessive water and mud. "The shoe pac was a high moccasin with a rubber foot and leather top, and the first model had 16 inch leather uppers." Combat testing at Anzio concluded that these boots were "indispensable in combating trench foot despite wet-mud conditions."[43] Dr. George Lytton, given a choice between wearing jumpboots or four-buckle rubber overshoes, declared that paratroopers in his regiment would not wear the four-buckle overshoes. When asked why they did not choose boots helpful in the prevention of trenchfoot, Lytton replied that it was a matter of pride to wear the jumpboots.[44]

Clogging the treads of combat boots is one way that mud affected military footwear. Mud trapped in a boot's tread causes a loss of traction and—depending on the type of mud—determines its trafficability. Type I and IIb's thickness causes the treads to clog, but even a small amount of slippery mud effectively reduces a boot's tractive function, often causing the combatant to slip or slide.

An initial attempt to increase the mobility of soldiers in mud was to create "mud shoes." By strapping boards to an infantryman's boots, the U.S. Army used the principle of spreading a soldier's weight over a large expanse of mud. Basically, the Army intended that "mud shoes" perform in mud as snowshoes do in snow. The trials did not encourage the issuance of mud shoes. In Vietnam, the U.S. military tried to resolve the mobility problem when it issued jungle boots. However, the first jungle boots had a Vibram-design sole with narrow grooves. This tread pattern allowed mud to accumulate in the narrow spaces. Another problem was the distance between the cleats in the sole and the heel where mud collected rather than dispersed. The solution to these problems came with the 1966 jungle boot, which featured "a Panama anti-mud traction design, replacing the earlier Vibram sole, which muddied too easily."[45]

In some conflicts, the quality of military footwear was so poor that boots and shoes disintegrated in the

Experimental mud shoes, Camp Gordon, January 1943.
National Archives

mud. Many soldiers, when conditions became so bad as to warrant it, improved their footwear with improvised methods. Williams noted such an instance during the American Civil War when he wrote: "Long marches over wet roads have destroyed fearfully the poor shoes issued by the government. I have at least 4,000 men in my division who are shoeless completely, or so nearly that they cannot march."[46] Most Confederate soldiers did not normally wear shoes and had never owned formal footwear.[47] Gen. James Longstreet, having many soldiers without shoes, told them to "take the rawhides of the beef cattle, killed for food; cut roughly for a moccasin-like covering for the feet, and there you are with something to walk in." However, this quick fix did not endure. "In the mud and icy slush of Virginia roads the moist, fresh skins slipped about as if on ice. The wearers, constantly up or down, finally kicked them aside and took the road as best they could." General Longstreet's aide, G. Moxley Sorrel, elaborating on the footwear issue, noted that a large number of shoes arrived from England, but they were "worthless, shoddy things." Sorrel admitted to wearing a pair, but "in a single day of wet and mud the cheats came to pieces."[48]

Mud has had a tremendous influence on casualty evacuation. Often the medical technology of a given period was sufficient to save wounded soldiers, but long delays in removing them from the battlefield cost lives. Although many factors hamper casualty evacuation, mud often inhibits stretcher bearers from rescuing wounded combatants in an efficient manner.

As warfare became a year-round event in the last 150 years, evacuating casualties has meant overcoming mud in a timely manner as time is a critical element in life saving. John Keegan asserted that "as many as a third of the 21,000 killed and missing on July 1 [1916] died as a result of wounds from which they would have had a chance of recovering" had they an opportunity for medical treatment within an hour or so of injury. One reason they did not have that opportunity was the relatively small number of stretcher bearers compared to the number of casualties. Keegan stated that a battalion "had thirty-two stretcher bearers, capable of carrying sixteen wounded between them, and needing an hour or more for each journey." However, it took precious time to recover more than three hundred wounded soldiers to the nearest aid station, the Regimental Aid Post. Moreover, soldiers at the Battle of the Somme, Keegan's subject, did not encounter the enormous quantities of mud that soldiers at Passchendaele did.[49]

Carrying a wounded soldier is hard enough under good field conditions, but in deep mud two men are not enough to act as stretcher bearers. British Army stretcher bearer Frank Dunham referred to an instance when he and his fellow SBs tried to move through a communication trench, which was thigh deep in mud: "All of us were constantly getting stuck in it and had to assist to pull each other out. Of course, we SBs had our 'well-beloved' stretcher to carry and this was well cursed before we reached our destination."[50] General Slim, quoting an official report, noted that mud made casualty evacuation so labor intensive that "half a company took ten hours to carry two stretcher cases four miles."[51] Sometimes sixteen men were necessary to carry one wounded man, and one stretcher bearer described it as the hardest work he ever performed. Cpl. Harold Chapin wrote in 1915 how his party of six evacuated two soldiers, "you have no idea of the physical fatigue entailed in carrying a twelve stone [wounded soldier] a thousand odd yards across muddy fields."[52] During World War II, a wounded American infantryman who stood 6 feet 2 inches tall and weighed 220 pounds felt guilty for the soldiers who evacuated him, saying that "I felt sorry for them having to carry me through that mud."[53]

Mud causes other difficulties for casualty evacuation, for instance, not enough stretcher bearers are available or they may be difficult to transport. Not only does a journey through mud take valuable lifesaving time from a wounded combatant but rarely is such a journey by stretcher a smooth one. No statistics exist indicating how many wounded soldiers suffered greater injury or died because of the rough journey, but Frank Dunham recalled that one soldier had a very rough "ride" back to the aid station because of the "slush and mud."[54] The U.S. Army's 133rd Infantry Regiment ordered many of its support personnel and its entire antitank company to act as stretcher bearers when the evacuation of wounded soldiers became impossible by vehicle.[55] In spring 1917, Siegfried Sassoon received a bullet wound to the shoulder blade. Not being a mortal wound nor inhibiting his ability to ambulate, Sassoon became one of the walking wounded and endured a 3-mile slog through the mud to reach the aid station.[56]

Stretcher parties are not the only means of casualty evacuation. Removal from the battlefield by horse-drawn ambulances was one historical method, but mud hinders horse and wagon as well as combatants. During the American Civil War, the enormous numbers of wounded soldiers proved difficult to evacuate. General Grant wrote of such a situation in May 1864 when his command suffered "five days of almost constant rain without any prospect of it clearing up. The roads have now become so impassable that ambulances with wounded men can no longer run between here and Fredericksburg."[57] Mud delayed the carts used by one British medical officer during World War I: "We pushed and heaved and attempted with the stretcher poles to lever out the wheels, but nothing happened. We left it in the mud."[58] A member of an Australian medical unit remembered, "Motor ambulances could not get through the churning mud, and the wagons needed four horses each but even then the animals quickly became exhausted."[59]

American units in World War II found tracked vehicles useful. In the Pacific Theater, the 321st Medical Battalion reported that each of its casualty-collecting platoons had three jeeps capable of accommodating four casualties, two on litters and two ambulatory cases, but more beneficial was each platoon's one M29c Weasel—a small fully tracked cargo carrier. As the American infantry advanced into the swampy interior of Leyte and roads disappeared, the 321st used shuttles of ambulances, hand carriers, and amphibious tractors to evacuate the wounded, but serious delays ranged from 1 to 30 hours in evacuating wounded soldiers.[60] When the M29c's broke down or mired in the mud, the battalion resorted to horses and hand-carry for evacuation. Regarding future operations, the 321st Medical Battalion advised that two M29c's per collecting platoon would make the difference.[61]

In other instances, even the M29c proved useless because of the small number of casualties it could carry and its "inability to negotiate heavy mud." As Okinawa's rainy season inundated the island with mud, roads failed, thus slowing casualty evacuation. "Coll [Collection] companies used Weasels (M29) entirely and they would not always get through." Eventually the 321st Medical Battalion had to use amphibious tractors to bypass the impassable roads evacuating the wounded from a clearing station to a land-based hospital.[62] The Ninety-sixth Infantry Division, which the 321st supported, reported that normally the estimated time of arrival for the wounded was just short of half an hour from the first line of medical facilities to the second, but it took another 40 minutes to evacuate casualties back to the clearing companies—the next level of medical care. When the rainy season hit, long hauls for stretcher teams were the norm, and the division had to borrow more powerful 2½-ton and M5 trucks, as they were the only vehicles that could handle the mud. "Under the most adverse conditions during the entire campaign the time lag from aid station to clearing station seldom exceeded six hours."[63] Admittedly, not all of these rare 6-hour transits was travel time, but even 4 to 5 hours from the time organized medical personnel first encountered the casualty to arrival at a field hospital was dangerous and mud was the cause.

Aircraft was another form of casualty evacuation intended to avoid Okinawa's mud. The First Marine Division found a solution to its evacuation difficulties using a paved road located within 400 yards of its collecting station and Cub airplanes to evacuate the wounded from the battlefield. These light aircraft evacuated 503 casualties to the division's field hospital, which had a purposely built Cub strip.[64]

CHAPTER 8

Mud, Fatigue,
Wear and Tear

"The snow and mud weighed heavy with every
step. . . . We had been thrust into hell, from
which there was no escape."[1]
—*Gottlob Herbert Bidermann*

While fighting in Vietnam, Army medic Daniel
Evans noted that mud was one of several factors
that induced fatigue: "Heat, humidity, water, mud, check-
ing one wood line after another–all of this contributed to
chronic fatigue among the troops."[2] Gerald Linderman
wrote in *The World Within War,* that fatigue is one of
three factors that makes combat veterans different from
other service members, inattentiveness and repetition
being the other two. Fighting, walking, and lying in mud
brings on fatigue, and although mud rarely, if ever, destroys a soldier's morale by itself, it can make life miserable.[3] In a study commissioned by the U.S. Army, Chester
McCall wrote in 1957 that fatigue was very difficult to
define but should include all instances of weariness
caused by such things as mud.[4] Fatigue affects combatants and it causes malfunctions in military equipment.

Mud causes fatigue in soldiers required to march and fight in it. Walking is not necessarily a strenuous activity. Simple bipedal motion does not cause fatigue in healthy human beings, which nearly all combatants are (or were before a lengthy campaign commenced). However, the depth of Type I and the adhesiveness of Type IIb muds in addition to their slippery quality inhibits normal walking and causes fatigue–and, in some cases, is indirectly responsible for a death.

During the American Civil War, General Williams wrote how a single day's plodding through rain and mud was "most fatiguing."[5] Lt. Erwin Rommel's company, after starting an early morning march in September 1914, waited for three hours because artillery and supply vehicles had become stuck in the mud and needed retrieving. Three hours later, the sun had risen, but the road was still in miserable shape from the traffic that crossed over it. As the company marched along the abysmal road, Rommel's soldiers pushed vehicles mired in the mud; and, for the first time, men fell out of a march because of fatigue. Even Rommel became weary, falling from his horse more than once as exhaustion overcame him. After marching for more than 15 hours, they finally rested. A combat march of such length was remarkable, but compounded the journey with mud capable of miring vehicles was a true feat of endurance.[6] E. B. Sledge described how "marching through Okinawa's mud" increased his exhaustion. He stated that normal walking "would try any man's patience, but in Okinawa's mud it drove us to a state of frustration and exasperation bordering on rage. It can be appreciated only by someone who has experienced it." He continued his diatribe on mud stating, "Mud just didn't interfere with vehicles. It exhausted the man on foot who was expected to keep on where wheels or treaded vehicles couldn't move."[7]

Type I mud also affects horses. At Passchendaele, deep churned-up mud required the use of four horses to pull every wagon, and exhaustion came quickly to these animals.[8] As horses became prime movers for the German army in November 1941, they suffered greatly from exhaustion as they hauled mired guns and vehicles through deep mud. The veterinarian of the German army's Thirtieth Infantry Division examined more than a thousand horses and determined that only a hundred had wounds while the rest suffered from exhaustion.[9]

Horses and mules also die from mud-induced exhaustion. Daniel Holt, a Union surgeon, recalled how three regimental horses died from pure exhaustion during the "Mud March."[10] Similarly, the mud near Chattanooga was so bad that "horses and mules sank to their bellies in place, which wore the animals out so much that many just laid down and died from sheer exhaustion."[11]

GIs versus mud on Hollandia, Dutch New Guinea, 1944.
National Archives

Soldiers and horses plying their way through a morass of Type IIb perform extra work causing greater exertion and subsequently immense physical exhaustion. Siegfried Sassoon related his exhaustion after leading a resupply party for 7 hours. "It rained all day and the trenches were a morass of glue-like mud. . . . I can believe that my party, staggering and floundering under its loads, would have made an impressive picture of 'Despair.'"[12] E. L. M. Burns wrote that burying cable was almost impossible at Passchendaele because "to struggle through the mud, lifting the clogging masses that attached themselves to the feet soon exhausted even the strongest men."[13] E. B. Sledge discovered this truth when ordered to dig a fighting position in late May 1945. He remembered that as other marines voiced their hatred of the mud and the smell of the battlefield, Sledge formed his fighting position using his shovel to move "heavy, sticky clay mud." The mud was so thick that Sledge stopped and removed the mud from each shovelful remarking, "I was thoroughly exhausted and thought my strength wouldn't last from one sticky shovelful to the next."[14]

Additionally, while soldiers and horses do not have to lift their feet out of slippery mud, the constant stumbling and fighting for balance exhausts them. At Soissons in mid-July 1918, a rain shower altered a road into ankle-deep mud and left already tired marines "slipping and staggering along like blind men."[15] General Slim stated that his soldiers were resilient, efficient, and capable of handling anything Burma threw at them, including the Japanese, but he admitted that his army had to slip and slide while marching on muddy roads.[16] Karl Fuchs told his wife that while fighting in the Soviet Union it was "very difficult to stay on your feet—that's how slippery it is."[17]

Walking in mud is bad enough, but attacking in muddy conditions is even worse. During an assault a soldier must maintain a steady, aggressive pace with enough ammunition and equipment to succeed. In earlier conflicts when victory over the enemy required soldiers to kill at close range, maintaining an adequate level of energy upon reaching the enemy was essential. In February 1593, Chinese cavalry became exhausted "as their horses bogged down in the mud" while fighting Japanese invaders in Korea.[18] At Agincourt, the attack of dismounted French knights began poorly as they ran across a plowed field toward the waiting English. By the time they reached the English position, fatigue was upon them and only a limited number of knights engaged the English because of the latter's narrow front. Mud had proved a crucial element as King Henry V's outnumbered English army held the field.[19] At the Battle of Waterloo, British cavalry who charged over churned up mud had difficulty returning, and fresh French cavalry began to catch their British counterparts. One of the victims was a British cavalry commander, Lord Ponsonby, easily ridden down and speared to death as lancers overtook him as his exhausted horse struggled with the mud.[20]

Good commanders consider exhaustion before ordering offensive actions. At times, the military situation demands that soldiers give their last reserves of energy, but when predicting how events might unfold, victorious leaders consider the present exhaustion of their troops. General Grant, knowing that the Confederates had retreated after the Battle of Shiloh over "almost impassable" roads after several days of frequent and heavy rain, did not order his soldiers to pursue as they had fought hard for two days, "lying in the mud and rain whenever not fighting."[21]

On the other hand, commanders during World War I did not always consider mud's exhaustive nature. According to the future Lieutenant General Burns, commanders overloaded the ordinary soldier with unnecessary equipment. Even with the additional burden, assaulting infantrymen needed to run or at least negotiate the terrain quickly, which was impossible in "ankle- or knee-deep sticky mud." Burns felt that these generals had served as courageous combat leaders in their early careers, but as warfare changed and their outlook on war had not, they "did not seem to be able to imagine the exhausting will-sapping effect of struggling through mud."[22]

Although World War I commanders did not consider the muddy terrain when they ordered an offensive, it became apparent as a battle continued that mud fatigued soldiers. Concerning the Battle of Passchendaele, Gen. Sir Hubert Gough, the commander of the British Fifth Army, realized that the infantry's progress would be so slow and fatiguing "that only the shortest advances could be contemplated." He knew that because of the

Even the versatile jeep had trouble with the mud of the Italian Front. November 1943, near Cassino. *U.S. Army Military History Institute*

mud the operation would fail or result in a Pyrrhic victory and recommended that the offensive end.[23] As the Battle of Passchendaele concluded, one British officer, looking over the muddy battlefield, exclaimed, "My God, did we really send men to fight in that?"[24] Burns wrote that attacking infantrymen needed all their energy for the eventual life and death struggle in the enemy trench. "If they are exhausted by struggling through mud, the drive to break through the enemy's resistance . . . will not be there."[25]

Regrettably, death from mud-induced exhaustion happened on more than one occasion. The physical toil required of soldiers who repeatedly raised their feet out of knee-deep quagmires proved to be too much for some individuals. What overcame some veterans was the overpowering weariness from long periods in deplorable conditions and the depletion of all physical reserves. The fatal exhaustion appeared more frequently in static fighting when the mental aspects of weariness deteriorated the willpower of combatants.

Major Grauwin recounted two instances when individuals died of exhaustion. Although mud, by itself, did not kill them, it was a significant factor. In the first instance, two men awaiting surgery died. Neither had wounds affecting any vital bones or organs, and Grauwin stated that neither their wounds nor anesthetic killed them. "They were dead simply because the heart and the vital functions had stopped as a result of compete physiological exhaustion." In the second incident, two legionnaires "collapsed in the mud with their burdens" after an arduous resupply detail. These two men died "from inanition, complete endocrine exhaustion" because of their extreme and constant physical exertion.[26]

Even relatively mundane and seemingly less hazardous work, such as that of a telephone linesman, when performed in large quantities of mud, brought emotional collapse from utter exhaustion. Burns recounted how on the Western Front in November 1916 a large man, tough and muscular, dropped the spool of cable he carried and collapsed in tears after a particularly hard struggle in the mud.[27]

Mud also causes wear and tear to vehicles and weapons. Mud's instability plagues transmissions, and Type I mud tears at vehicle parts such as tires, CV (constant velocity) joints and boots, brakes, and brakelines. And more recovery operations are necessary as vehicles either break down or become mired. Mud also affects weapons. As mentioned previously, the recoil of cannons and mortars in mud causes inaccuracies, and large quantities of Type I and Type IIb mud clog the inner workings of small arms.

Three mechanical parts that pay a heavy price in especially thick mud are a vehicle's brakes, tires, and transmission. Tires, although they do not always fail, lose their efficiency. Like the soles of boots that gum up with mud and lose their tractive ability, vehicles that acquire enough thick mud lose the gripping force of their tires. Guy Sajer recalled how the truck he drove in 1942 exhausted the tractive function of its tires and required towing. "Our truck, whose wheels by this time were balls of mud, was pulled forward, while its engine rattled helplessly."[28] In addition, General Rendulic recalled that deep mud created a greater demand for gasoline and placed an enormous load on the engine.[29] The constant shifting and sudden loss of torque when tires broke free from mud took a toll on the gears. For example, the heavy mud found in Italy during October 1944 degraded the vehicles in the U.S. Army's Thirty-fourth Infantry Division. The division reported that a high percentage of its trucks broke down as mud destroyed brakes and transmissions.[30] General Guderian also noted that tanks used to recover vehicles (a task not specifically designed for tanks to accomplish) rapidly wore out their transmissions in October 1941.[31]

Other parts of motor vehicles prone to failure in excessive mud are those found under the frame. Horse-drawn wagons are another victim of mud-induced failure. General Williams told his daughter of an experience he had in late November 1861, "I found lots of mule wagons stalled in the mud, some with broken tongues and others badly disabled in other ways."[32] During World War II, members of the U.S. Army's 133rd Infantry Regiment welded extensions to the exhaust pipes of their 2½-ton cargo trucks "to prevent mud from clogging the exhaust exit."[33] Large quantities of Type I mud wore away at CV joints' protective boots. Lt. Lamar Myers recalled just how destructive mud was to the vehicles in his engineer company in Vietnam. He noted that in terms of the vehicle's body and frame, they "held up better than you would ever expect, but the soft things on a vehicle—CV joints, CV boots, brakes, and things of that nature" often broke in Type I mud. Constant use in deep mud wore the boots out, and when mud eventually penetrated the CV joint through the torn boot, it corrupted the joint causing its failure. Mud-induced wear on CV joints meant that Myers's engineers replaced them more than once a week. If his company were back in the United States, Myers noted, a vehicle might survive for a couple of years without a new CV joint, but in Vietnam's mud replacements were necessary.[34]

Vehicle maintenance attributable to mud's effects caused delays on Myers's missions. He explained that although he might start with all of his vehicles one morning, after using them all day and servicing them through the night, he might have only 90 percent of his vehicles available for the next day. Every day he would lose a percentage of the remainder as long as the operation continued. Finally, he recalled either having to "scream uncle and ask for more vehicles or have a stand down" so that his unit could perform the needed repairs.[35]

Myers knew that excessive vehicle maintenance affected his men. What physically drained his soldiers was the toll mud took on their equipment and the great amount of physical labor demanded of combat engineers. These already exhausted soldiers performed more maintenance than they would have under drier circumstances. Myers stated that if the soldier "who is driving the truck in the daytime is the same man who is pulling maintenance at night, trying to eat and sleep in between, you know the guy is fatigued."[36]

Vehicles that break down because of mud's influence rarely do it in a clean, dry environment and require recovery. Belton Cooper recalled how recovery teams prioritized their efforts, "They first went for the tanks

U.S. Army truck attempting to leave base camp in Vietnam during Operation Manhattan, May 1967. *Ivyl Myers*

that were merely stuck in the mud, because they had their tracks intact and were easier to pull out."[37] Lieutenant Carius remembered, "Wheeled vehicles sank up to their axles and we were afraid that our tanks would sink to their hulls." When trucks mired to such depths, they mired because "mud dammed up in front of the radiators." Not wanting to leave the trucks behind, Tiger tank crews placed "one to two trucks in tow." To make matters worse, "if the tow cable was strong enough, it ripped out the truck's front axle along with its wheels." When Carius reached his destination, a train station, "most of the vehicles were ready for the repair shop."[38] Lamar Myers remembered moving immobilized vehicles through a muddy region of Vietnam using truck winches almost entirely. His engineers attached the vehicle's winch to a tree, hauled the truck forward, detached the cable from that tree, attached it to another tree further forward and repeated the process until the truck was clear of the mud.[39] When a winch was not available, rope was the answer. Heinz Guderian, encountering the *rasputiza* for the first time in 1941, remembered that wheeled vehicles required the assistance of tanks to move, but not enough chains existed so aircraft dropped rope to the hundreds of mired vehicles, a mission that took the Luftwaffe more than a week to accomplish.[40]

Bulldozers are a common means for retrieving vehicles stuck in the mud. Designed for use in muddy conditions, they proved essential to mission accomplishment on more than one occasion. In its report following the Ryukyus Campaign, one infantry regiment praised the work of Company A, 321st Engineers. The engineers did their best to keep the roads open, thus enhancing support missions. "When the roads were impassable, in many cases, to wheeled vehicles, the engineers spotted bulldozers at all the bad spots and pulled our supply vehicles through."[41] However, bulldozers were not immune to the powerful effects of mud in combination with steep slopes. In Italy, a bulldozer attached to the 133rd Infantry Regiment was unable to reach its assigned destination because the hill it had to cross was "too steep and slippery" with 200 yards of mud 2 feet deep.[42]

Sometimes even two bulldozers are not enough to retrieve a tracked vehicle. To recover a deeply mired M48 tank from an abandoned rice paddy, Lieutenant Myers tried using a bulldozer to recover the stricken vehicle. However, all the bulldozer did was churn the soft soil around the tank. As a solution, Myers brought in two more bulldozers and had each winch out its cable to maximum length in an effort to find stable ground. The two bulldozers hooked to the first one and all of them began pulling, trying to retrieve one tank stuck deeply in the mud. In the end, he abandoned the tank.[43]

Before the Gunpowder Age, mud never seriously hindered the effectiveness of edged weapons or missiles systems. (In some instances, mud surely caused a combatant's hand to slip on a sword hilt or fouled a bowstring, but it did not truly blunt the weapon's ability to do harm.) As gunpowder weapons became more complex with increasingly smaller and delicate parts, mud's ability to affect their use increased, but mud first hindered weapons when artillery became more prominent. Although catapults, ballistas, and such weapons existed before the fifteenth century, they were not truly mobile weapons systems and more often were constructed on site. As artillery became more mobile, mud affected it. For an artillery battalion fighting on World War II's Gothic Line, moving guns was extremely difficult because the area of operation was a quagmire of mud.[44]

In terms of weapon effectiveness, the bane of ground combatants is thick mud's ability to clog the inner mechanisms of small arms. The situation of inoperable weapons during World War I became such a common occurrence that soldiers took to bayonets and grenades as the only reliable weapons.[45] While fighting for Vimy Ridge, Burns ordered a Lewis gunner to clean a gun when Burns found it "covered with mud and out of action."[46] Mud-fouled rifles and machine guns could mean life or death on the battlefield. The American 334th Infantry Regiment reported in November 1944 that large amounts of mud caused many weapons to jam.[47] Small arms clogged with mud threatened victory on the battlefield. During World War I, British weapons "became so choked with mud that it was impossible to use them when the enemy counterattacked," and one British officer remarked,

Mud flotation adapters, shown attached to the wheels of a jeep, were designed by a captain in the 981st Regiment Maintenance Company to combat the deep mud often prevalent on the front, January 1945. *National Archives*

"You can't clean a rifle when your hands are covered an inch thick." Gen. Erich von Ludendorff stated that as small arms jammed with mud and stopped functioning, victory went to the side with the most soldiers. "As the mud became worse, the task of keeping weapons clean and serviceable became more and more difficult and was an important element in bringing operations to a close."[48]

Mud was one reason for a French machine rifle's reputation for unreliability. The Chauchat machine rifle did not operate well in World War I's extremely muddy conditions. The notoriety of this weapon's poor performance was such that in May 1917 Gen. Henri Pétain sent questionnaires to all French units in the field concerning the Chauchat. According to the written response of the 398th Infantry Division "mud is enemy No. 1 of the gun; when it gets in, which is difficult to avoid, the weapon becomes inoperative." Four other French infantry divisions and two infantry regiments also reported difficulties with the weapon and the ceaseless mud. The combat surveys determined that the guns jammed because their magazines had "four major wide-open areas through which mud and dirt could enter, thus clogging the mechanism."[49]

Because of the numerous weapon malfunctions, World War I combatants devised measures to prevent mud-induced stoppages. French soldiers temporarily solved the problem by urinating "in their rifles to release the mechanism."[50] Another method of preventing stoppages was to cover one's weapon. The Chauchat machine rifle's problems with mud became so pervasive that later issues of the weapon came with a protective bag. Admittedly, this alleviated problems in its magazine and inner mechanism, but removing the weapon from its protective sheath in a combat situation could cost the life of the operator and it did not prevent mud from entering the weapon once it was in use. British soldiers fighting in Flanders during World War I also used cloth to keep their weapons' inner mechanisms free of mud, but doing so did not leave the weapon ready for immediate use.[51]

During World War II, Sten guns were manufactured by the thousands, both in the United States and Britain. The simplest British version contained only forty-seven different parts and was made of pressed metal components. Although a popular weapon because it could be produced fast and inexpensively, it also had a reputation with troops as crude and unreliable, sometimes discharging if knocked or dropped. Additionally, the Sten rounds fed into the magazine by merging into a single column. Dirt and mud could enter this area and jam the mechanism.[52] Because of this, newer 9mm magazines are curved and feed from both sides of the weapon, avoiding possibility of mud malfunction.

CHAPTER 9

Forever Mud

Noted contemporary author Kurt Vonnegut knew the significance of mud. In his novel *Cat's Cradle*, a Marine general approaches a scientist with a potential war-winning idea: he proposes that wars will end faster with fewer casualties if a process is developed to harden mud instantly. Historians have not recognized what Vonnegut and soldiers knew: the importance of mud on military operations.

Will there always be mud on the battlefield? The seemingly obvious answer is, of course. Mud has historically played a significant role. And its emotional and physical impact on combatants will not dry up in the near future.

"American Tanks Stuck in Mud!" This headline could have appeared in American newspapers if Coalition forces had not planned appropriately for the permanent mud of Iraq's marshes during the 2003 invasion. Although the Coalition advance to Baghdad did not lose much momentum to mud, commanders knew it existed and avoided it, thereby depriving Iraqi defenders of a chance to inflict greater damage. During the 1991 Gulf War, Iraq had demonstrated its willingness to use the environment as a weapon when it destroyed numerous oil wells in Kuwait and released oil into the Persian Gulf. What might Iraqi forces do this time to an army invading their country?[1]

Coalition planners realized that Iraqi leaders might order flooding of parts of their country to stall the allies's advance. The U.S. Marine Corps took such a threat seriously and organized the knowledge of many experts from fields such as engineering, hydrology, meteorology, and remote sensing to determine what areas would be most susceptible to intentional flooding. The Marine Corps Intelligence Activity (MCIA) produced several hundred cartographic products that depicted how water bodies and mud might hinder the invasion. It developed such terrain analyses as "cross-country mobility, vegetation and wetness change detection, slope, three-dimensional perspective views, surface drainage analyses, lines of communications studies and interactive terrain flythroughs on video." In addition, the MCIA discovered how the British had surrendered in 1916 after an early spring thaw had caused the Tigris River to rise and flood, preventing the British from receiving additional food, materials, or troops. Although the Iraqis had not intentionally flooded their country then, mud did influence at least one encounter during the invasion.[2]

In March 2003, mud played a role in the Battle of An Nasiriyah. What commanders intended to be the rapid seizure of two key bridges became one of the fiercest battles of the war. The marines of Task Force Tarawa believed that it was important to cross the Euphrates River at An Nasiriyah immediately, without really knowing what the terrain was like on the other side. Time was critical, and to wait for reinforcements might mean fighting for the bridges in the dark.[3]

From preinvasion intelligence and some firsthand experience, Coalition forces knew that the terrain surrounding permanent roads was potentially muddy and capable of slowing, if not stopping, their vehicles. For example, at least one road near the fighting at An Nasiriyah was flanked by "swampy irrigation ditches." Leading the assault on the bridges at An Nasiriyah was Company B of the First Battalion Second Marine Regiment (1/2), which was to support the main attack of C Company also from 1/2. The initial plan was for those units advancing over the Euphrates River Bridge to turn right immediately after crossing to avoid attacking into an ambush-rich, urban environment. The problem was that the terrain immediately off the bridge was Type I mud.

Gy.Sgt. Randy Howard, the commander of the lead tank, realized, however, that the roadway leading down from the bridge did not permit an immediate right turn. In fact, to turn right, he first had to turn left and then double back on himself. Worrying about the close proximity of houses and low-hanging electrical wires and wary of exposing his tank to multiple flank shots from Iraqi gunners, he decided to proceed ahead on "Ambush Alley" into An Nasiriyah and seek another route to the right. After moving three blocks into the city, he turned down a very narrow street, which gave way to an open area, nearly 200 meters long, of what appeared to be firmly compacted mud. Howard had found a route that bypassed the city, but he did not notice until too late just what the terrain was really like.

Before he knew it, Howard's tank was stuck in the mud. His driver tried to work the tank from its predicament, but the churning of its treads only dug the tank in deeper. Following behind Howard was S.Sgt. Dominic Dillon's tank, which also quickly mired. A third tank led by Gy.Sgt. George Insko tried to "maneuver over what he was sure was hard-packed mud." It too sank into the quagmire, but Insko managed to alert the fourth tank led by S.Sgt. Aaron Harrell to stay out of it.

Having been a tanker for nearly a decade, Harrell had recovered numerous tanks from many situations, but the scene at An Nasiriyah was unlike any he could recall. He too had originally believed that what the other three tanks had entered was hard-packed mud, but he soon realized that the other tanks were entering "a bog of watery mud and sewage." All the tanks, except his, were in thick Type I mud up to the tops of the treads. Two more tracked vehicles and several Humvees were soon stuck, as well. In an attempt to get out of the mud, the tank drivers gunned their engines hoping and praying that the tread could get a grip on something—anything—and pull them from their precarious position. Crewmen waded into the mud in an attempt to retrieve their vehicles. Cpl. Neville Welch witnessed one marine attach a recovery rope to a mired amphibious assault vehicle. The marine secured the line, but the mud nearly swallowed him, and fellow marines had to retrieve him from rescuing his own track.[4]

The advance had been brought "to a sudden halt as the apparently firm ground turned out to be a thick muddy bog disguised by a thin crust of hardened dirt." How the mud came to be there is still open to question. In *An Nasiriyah*, Gary Livingston recalled that a thin layer of dirt deceptively covered the mud. However, S.Sgt. Troy Schielein believed that the area had been flooded intentionally. "They knew we were mechanized and they wanted to slow us down." Others thought that the huge muddy expanse resulted from sewer run-off.[5]

Within 3 to 4 minutes, nearly half of Company B was stuck. The other half, at least one complete platoon, had to proceed with the mission, which was to support Company C's crossing of the other bridge. However, mud had changed the tactical situation. As half of the company continued the mission, the rest remained mired —exactly the kind of situation Central Command wanted to avoid. "Because of the mud stuck vehicles, Bravo Company would have to fight their way out to accomplish their mission of supporting Charlie Company's attack to secure the second bridge."

Capt. Tim Newland, the commander of Company B called up a tank retriever, and after 4 hours it rescued the tanks and tracks. The commanders decided to leave the tank retriever and two of the Humvees and continue on with their mission as best they could. Luckily, their misadventure with the stinking quagmire did not cost Company B any life-threatening casualties "except to their pride at being partially stuck and mucking around in the muddy sewer."[6]

Mud has influenced battles in the past as well as the present, and mud will continue to have a role in future conflicts. With increased urbanization throughout the world, there has been a decline in muddy battlefields. But military planners still must give mud its full respect; in some instances they are learning.

The controversy concerning armored Humvees in Iraq does not seem to consider the vehicle's performance in mud. The losses of people and vehicles from improvised explosive devices (IEDs) in Iraq compelled the up-armoring of vehicles, especially thin-skinned Humvees. No one faults the men and women or their higher commands for trying to protect themselves, but how has adding armor to the vehicles changed their operational limitations?

Add-on armor can increase the weight of a vehicle from 1,000 to 4,000 pounds. One liability of additional armor is the additional wear and tear on engines, suspensions, and transmissions. These critical automotive components, although they may tolerate the increase, were not designed for the additional weight.[7] In addition, the added weight may be one of many factors responsible for a significant increase in the number of rollovers.[8] Without knowing the full details, soldiers are unprepared when the soft walls of canal and irrigation ditches cannot support the weight of these heavier vehicles. Additionally, the extra weight makes the vehicles much more susceptible to mud. Humvees, when 2,000 pounds lighter, might be more resilient to mud. Again, no one wants to face the increased danger from IEDs, but does the military consider mud in its equations?

Fortunately, the military has begun to take mud into account. One of the more apparent instances is in equipment testing. The U.S. Army at Aberdeen Proving Grounds uses muddy areas to test equipment. Personnel put vehicles through a tough set of tests, including a mud pool, to determine how well potentially new pieces of equipment tolerate the mud. Researchers at Aberdeen have noted that devising standard soil parameters to test a vehicle's trafficability is difficult—if not impossible—to measure directly.[9]

The U.S. Air Force also considers future uses of mud. A research paper written by Air Force officers titled "Weather as a Force Multiplier: Owning the Weather in 2025" is a shortened version of a two-year study conducted by the Air War College. The paper concentrates on how weather might affect Air Force operations and considers how changing the weather can either increase or decrease the amount of mud on a battlefield. Besides emphasizing weather's role in air operations, it considers the influence that mud might have on future battlefields. Specifically, it looks at ways in which weather can be altered to either degrade enemy force or enhance the operational capabilities of friendly forces. To degrade an enemy's operational capabilities via increased rain and mud, the paper suggests flooding lines of communication, reducing reconnaissance effectiveness, and decreasing the comfort level and morale of enemy troops. In terms of enhancing the operational capabilities of friendly forces, the paper's authors believe that if they can control the weather, precipitation avoidance would be beneficial. With less rain would come less mud, and friendly forces could either maintain or improve the lines of communication and maintain the comfort level and morale of U.S. forces.[10]

To either degrade or enhance military operations, the paper points out that although precipitation may affect different types of operations, "ground mobility is most affected." Mud, through increased precipitation, will reduce the mobility of the enemy and detrimentally affect its morale. Conversely, if weather modification suppresses potential precipitation, the lack of mud might aid the trafficability of friendly forces. The ideal method to cause rain is to use carbon black dust above a large water body upwind from the intended target area. Solar energy drawn to the black dust heats the surrounding air and increases the evaporation of the water body. In addition, "parcels of air will rise and the water vapor contained in the rising air parcel will eventually condense to form clouds." As the air mass moves downwind toward the target area, droplets within the cloud will increase and become too heavy for the air mass. Precipitation will then fall, and mud will form.[11]

Although mud has influenced campaigns and battles, for the most part mud is an inconvenience, and senior military commanders are not making any noticeable effort to diminish its appearance on the battlefield. However, the armed services are making inroads. For example, the U.S. Navy has increased its use of hovercraft or landing craft, air cushioned (LCACs), in part to cope with tidal swamps and mudflats that occur all over the globe. Aircraft do not readily come to mind when someone considers mud's influence on military operations, but aircraft sometimes must take off and land on muddy airstrips. Pilots of cargo aircraft such as the C-130 must have the versatility of landing on forward unpaved airstrips. The U.S. Air Force has means for rating landing conditions based on many factors, and the status of the soil on makeshift airfields is one they must consider. The Marine Corps, in an attempt to keep feet dry and boots where they belong, has expressed interest in waders "designed to keep the feet locked in while wading through muddy or swampy areas."[12]

Mud still occurs on the battlefield and will appear in future conflicts. Although not all combatants have encountered mud during their military service, if they dealt with any significant quantities of it, then they often remembered the experience vividly. On February 21, 1951, U.S. marines believed that "the gods of Korea, it seemed, had decreed that everyone taking part in Operation Killer was going to have some lasting memories of mud."[13] Writing about the Reichswald offensive, General Horrocks proclaimed, "I am certain that this must be the chief memory of everyone who fought in the Reichswald battle. Mud and still more mud."[14] Writing about the same battle in his account of the Ninth Royal Tank Regiment (RTR), Peter Beale noted that "most people remembered one thing about Geilenkirchen—mud."[15]

Most soldiers wished that they had a miracle invention that could either evaporate or freeze mud and rid them of the trials and tribulations that saturated soil entailed. If such a miracle device could work, then combatants would never again struggle through the muck or endure mud's discomfort and misery. Marines and soldiers would no longer suffer health complications or the loss of vehicles or weapons malfunction if mud disappeared entirely from future battlefields. The armed services have only recently begun to see, as did Vonnegut's fictional general, that mud can be a very significant factor of success or failure on the battlefield.

APPENDIX

Table 1
SELECTED SOIL CHARACTERISTICS[1]

	Predominantly Gravel	Predominantly Sand
Dry	Solid	Loose
	Stable	Unstable
Wet	Solid	Compact
	Stable	Stable
Frost	Unaffected	Unaffected

	Predominantly Silt	Predominantly Clay
Dry	Compact	Hard
	Dusty	Dusty
Wet	Spongy	Sticky
	Slippery	Slippery
	Fast Drying	Slow Drying
Frost	Heaves	Heaves

Table 2
Mud in Relation to Operations when Accomplishment of Operation was Prevented[2]

Type of Operation	Number/ Percentage of Incidents Reported	Rank
Aircraft	10/5	
Armor	67/35	1
Heavy Weapons	17/9	
Small Arms	11/6	
Complex[3]	24/12	3
Amphibious	1/1	
Engineer	6/3	1
General and Individual[4]	0/0	
Medical	1/1	1
Ordnance	2/1	3
Signal	0/0	
Transportation	54/28	

The first number is the actual count of incidents reported for that type of operation, and the second number is the percentage presented by that count. The third column ranks mud among other environmental factors for that operation.

Table 3
MUD IN RELATION TO OPERATIONS WHEN ACCOMPLISHMENT OF OPERATION WAS DELAYED OR OBSTRUCTED[5]

Type of Operation	Number/ Percentage of Incidents Reported	Rank
Aircraft	6/1	
Armor	114/14	1
Heavy Weapons	83/10	
Small Arms	30/4	
Complex	177/22	1
Amphibious	1/0	
Engineer	17/2	1
General and Individual	20/2	1
Medical	39/5	1
Ordnance	14/2	1
Signal	6/1	
Transportation	294/37	1

The first number is the actual count of incidents reported for that type of operation, and the second number is the percentage presented by that count. The third column ranks mud among other environmental factors for that operation.

NOTES

Introduction

1. Burns, *General Mud*, 21.
2. Campbell, "The Environmental Element in Military Operations," 13.

Chapter 1:
Mud's Types, Characteristics, and Effects

1. Johnson, *Battlefields of the World War*, 109. For this section see Collins, *Military Geography*, 36–39; and Winters et al., *Battling the Elements*, 33–34.
2. Fritz, *Frontsoldaten*, 74. While learning to recover vehicles in deep mud, a fellow student had a pair of expensive sunglasses drop from his face into the mud. Even though he grasped for them within seconds, he could not find them after several minutes of searching (author's note).
3. Collins, *Military Geography*, 36, 38.
4. Stamp, ed., *A Glossary of Geographical Terms*, 330.
5. U.S. Marine Corps, *Small Unit Leader's Guide to Weather and Terrain*, B-12; and Winters et al., *Battling the Elements*, 33.
6. Collins, *Military Geography*, 36. Mud is too complicated for such a simple definition. Compaction, layering, and angularity are among the variables that differentiate between wet soil and mud. Any more elaborate attempt at defining mud is beyond the scope of this book and its examination of how mud influences warfare.
7. Gregory, ed., *Military Geology and Topography,* 59.
8. The History of the 808th Engineer Aviation Battalion, RG 407.

9. Collins, *Military Geography*, 36–37.
10. Gregory, ed., *Military Geology and Topography*, 59.
11. The History of the 808th Engineer Aviation Battalion, RG 407.
12. Horrocks, *A Full Life*, 141.
13. Burns, *News Hour with Jim Lehrer*.
14. Conroy, *Heavy Metal*, 119.
15. War Department, "Low Pressure Tires in Mud," 4.
16. Doolittle, "Jimmy Doolittle: The Man Behind the Legend," 41.
17. Evans and Sasser, *Doc*, 190.
18. Myers, Warren, et al., eds., *An Informal History of the 631st Field Artillery Battalion*, 70.
19. Towne, *Doctor Danger Forward*, 123.
20. Fuchs, *Sieg Heil*, 145.
21. Bidermann, *In Deadly Combat*, 99.
22. Leinbaugh and Campbell, *The Men of Company K*, 228.
23. Sledge, *With the Old Breed*, 208.
24. Leinbaugh and Campbell, *The Men of Company K*, 44.
25. Herringham, *A Physician in France*, 238.
26. War Department, "Low Pressure Tires in Mud," 4.
27. Burns, *General Mud*, 25.
28. Frank Fox, *The Battle of the Ridges,* 95, quoted in Johnson, *Battlefields of the World War,* 24.
29. Mallonee, "One Man's War," 18.
30. Sajer, *The Forgotten Soldier*, 86–87, 92.
31. Beale, *Tank Tracks*, 50.
32. Dunham, *The Long Carry*, 118.
33. Department of the Army, *Terrain Factors in the Russian Campaign*, 20.
34. Fuchs, *Sieg Heil*, 147, 137.
35. History, 133rd Infantry, October 1944.
36. O'Sullivan, *Terrain and Tactics*, 120; and Collins, *Military Geography*, 37.
37. Winters et al., *Battling the Elements*, 89.
38. Action Against Enemy Report, 321st Engineer Battalion, RG 407.
39. Burns, *General Mud*, ix.
40. Strahler and Donaldson, "Objective and Quantitative Field Methods of Terrain Analysis," 13; Collins, *Military Geog-*

raphy, 37; and O'Sullivan, *Terrain and Tactics*, 120. Conversely, Arthur Strahler and Koons Donaldson's study on terrain analysis suggests that some soils find greater strength when "agitated and compacted under load." This strength derives from the "closer packing of the mineral grains, increasing the internal cohesion and interparticle friction." (Strahler and Donaldson, "Objective and Quantitative Field Methods of Terrain Analysis," 13.)

41. Keegan, *The Face of Battle*, 143.
42. Rendulic, *Battle in Mud*, 1.
43. Bryant, *Sekigahara 1600*, 51–52.
44. Sassoon, *Memoirs of an Infantry Officer*, 85.
45. Department of the Army, "Terrain Factors in the Russian Campaign," 11.
46. Von Senger und Etterlin, "March of an Armored Division during the Muddy Season," 100.
47. Turnbull, *The Samurai*, 224.
48. Howarth, *A Near Run Thing*, 177.
49. Burns, *General Mud*, 21.
50. Carius, *Tigers in the Mud*, 220.
51. Williams, *From the Cannon's Mouth*, 107.
52. Rommel, *Attacks*, 44, 169. See also Howard, *The Franco-Prussian War*, 109, 160; and Leinbaugh and Campbell, *The Men of Company K*, 54.
53. *Congressional Medal of Honor Library, 125.*
54. Linderman, *The World Within War*, 282.
55. Grauwin, *Doctor at Dienbienphu*, 261, 182.
56. Howarth, *A Near Run Thing*, 89.
57. Isaacs, "Tough Old Gut—Italy, November 1942–June 1944."
58. Rendulic, *Battle in Mud*, 6.
59. Thucydides, *The Peloponnesian War*, 173.
60. Cerasini, *Heroes*, 197.
61. Dunham, *The Long Carry*, 118.
62. Cooper, *Death Traps*, 151–152.
63. Hamric, interview.
64. Jones, interview.
65. Drea, "A Very Savage Operation," 49.
66. Kennedy and Park, "The Army Green Uniform."
67. Nunneley and Tamayama, *Tales by Japanese Soldiers*, 33, 144.

68. Jones, interview.
69. Grauwin, *Doctor at Dienbienphu*, 256.
70. Metelmann, *Through Hell for Hitler*, 59.
71. Grauwin, *Doctor at Dienbienphu*, 182.
72. *The Wipers Times*, 313.

Chapter 2: Permanent Mud

1. Sun-tzu, *The Art of War*, 104.
2. See Collins, *Military Geography*, 122–126.
3. Monkhouse, *A Dictionary of Geography*, 340, 424.
4. Markey, *From Iowa to the Philippines*, 234.
5. Isaacs, "The Desert—North Africa, 1940–1943."
6. Department of the Army, *Terrain Analysis*, Intro 6–7.
7. O'Sullivan and Miller, *The Geography of Warfare*, 57.
8. Jones, *The Art of War in the Western World,* 157–159.
9. Petre, *Napoleon's Campaign in Poland, 1806–1807*, 110.
10. Burns, *General Mud*, 56–57, 73.
11. Carius, *Tigers in the Mud*, 85.
12. Remini, *The Battle of New Orleans*, 84.
13. Reilly, *The British at the Gates*, 261; and Remini, *The Battle of New Orleans*, 84.
14. Remini, *The Battle of New Orleans*, 93.
15. Ibid., 85.
16. Reilly, *The British at the Gates*, 262, 274.
17. Remini, *The Battle of New Orleans*, 276, 281, 92, 93.
18. Ibid., 113–115.
19. Ibid., 110.
20. Reilly, *The British at the Gates*, 289, 290, 298.
21. Remini, *The Battle of New Orleans*, 150.
22. Cooper, *Death Traps*, 308.
23. Murray and Millett, *A War to Be Won*, Appendix 3, 598.
24. Cooper, *Death Traps*, 24, 229, 152, 26, 211, 139.
25. Koschorrek, *Blood Red Snow*, 158, 160.
26. Cooper, *Death Traps*, 140–141.
27. Ibid., 90, 147–148.
28. Elstob, *Battle of the Reichswald*, 90.
29. Leinbaugh and Campbell, *The Men of Company K*, 106.
30. Herringham, *A Physician in France*, 221.
31. Johnson, *Battlefields of the World War*, 66.
32. Slim, *Defeat into Victory,* 350, 362; and Myers, interview.

33. Myers, interview.
34. Gilmore and Davis, *A Connecticut Yankee in the 8th Gurkha Rifles*, 150.
35. Leinbaugh and Campbell, *The Men of Company K*, 106.
36. S-3 Periodic Report, Headquarters First Battalion 135th Infantry, RG 407; and Johnson, *Battlefields of the World War*, 66.
37. Williams, *From the Cannon's Mouth*, 38.
38. Stone, "Army Mission Quickly Turns into Quagmire," 3A.
39. Burns, "1863: Simply Murder."
40. Bevilacqua, "Operation Killer," 16.

Chapter 3: Seasonal Mud

1. Department of the Army, *Military Improvisations during the Russian Campaign*, 3.
2. Slim, *Defeat into Victory*, 496.
3. Glantz and House, *When Titans Clashed*, 80.
4. Winters et al., *Battling the Elements*, 87. See also chapter 4, "Invading Another Climate as Seasons Change." One benefit of invading Russia during the early summer was that "localized swamplands were less a problem in summer, and with care some could even be traversed." (Winters et al., *Battling the Elements*, 89) Even the vast Pripet marshes, which the Germans avoided, were less of a threat in the summer than during the *rasputiza*.
5. Department of the Army, *Military Improvisations during the Russian Campaign*, 1.
6. Showalter, "Operation Barbarossa," 47–48.
7. Von Senger und Etterlin, "March of an Armored Division during the Muddy Season," 100.
8. Showalter, "Operation Barbarossa," 47–48.
9. Rendulic, *Battle in Mud*, 2–3.
10. Guderian, *Panzer Leader*, 233–234, 224–225.
11. Wilhelm Prüller quoted in Fritz, *Frontsoldaten*, 105.
12. "The Invasion of Russia."
13. Department of the Army, *Military Improvisations during the Russian Campaign*, 3.
14. O'Sullivan, *Terrain and Tactics*, 115.
15. Showalter, "Operation Barbarossa," 47–48.
16. Isaacs, "Barbarossa, June–December 1941."

17. Winters et al., *Battling the Elements*, 89–90.
18. Fuchs, *Sieg Heil*, 148n.
19. Guderian, *Panzer Leader*, 244.
20. Murray and Millett, *A War to Be Won*, 133–134.
21. Isaacs, "Barbarossa, June–December 1941."
22. Guderian, *Panzer Leader*, 245.
23. Murray and Millett, *A War to Be Won*, 398.
24. Rendulic, *Battle in Mud*, 1–2.
25. Bidermann, *In Deadly Combat*, 280.
26. Glantz and House, *When Titans Clashed*, 114.
27. Murray and Millett, *A War to Be Won*, 398–399.
28. Jennewein, "Survival in the Wilderness," 58.
29. Murray and Millett, *A War to Be Won*, 398.
30. Von Senger und Etterlin, "March of an Armored Division during the Muddy Season," 102–104.
31. Ibid., 105–106.
32. Murray and Millett, *A War to Be Won*, 398. Several sources refer to these animals, but it is not clear whether they were horses or ponies. Gottlob Bidermann described the animals he encountered as "Ukrainian ponies" (Bidermann, *In Deadly Combat*, 62), while R. L. DiNardo's study of horses in the German army stated that "the most common horses found in the Soviet Union proper were the panje horses" (DiNardo, *Mechanized Juggernaut or Military Anachronism*, 46).
33. DiNardo, *Mechanized Juggernaut or Military Anachronism*, 90; and Rendulic, *Battle in Mud*, 3.
34. Department of the Army, *Military Improvisations during the Russian Campaign*, 52–53.
35. Ibid., 12–13; and Department of the Army, *Terrain Factors in the Russian Campaign*, 15.
36. Showalter, "Operation Barbarossa," 47–48.
37. DiNardo, *Mechanized Juggernaut or Military Anachronism*, 46.
38. Monkhouse, *A Dictionary of Geography*, 232. For this section, see Collins, *Military Geography*, 375–376.
39. Gilmore and Davis, *A Connecticut Yankee in the 8th Gurkha Rifles*, 151–152.
40. Slim, *Defeat into Victory*, 99, 109.
41. Ibid., 291–292, 400; and Gilmore and Davis, *A Connecticut Yankee in the 8th Gurkha Rifles*, 179.

42. Slim, *Defeat into Victory*, 277–278; and Smith, "The Chindits Heroic Sacrifice at Blackpool," 53.

43. Slim, *Defeat Into Victory*, 480, 483, 505.

44. The History of the 808th Engineer Aviation Battalion, RG 407.

45. Moore, *A Dictionary of Geography*, 138.

46. Yahara, *The Battle for Okinawa*, 83.

47. Ibid., 94.

48. Myers, Warren, et al., eds., *An Informal History of the 631st Field Artillery Battalion*, 73. Maj.Gen. Sir Kenneth Strong remembered a comment some Russian officers visiting Italy in December 1943 made: "The mud in Italy was worse than anything they had experienced in Russia." (Strong, *Intelligence at the Top*, 169–170.)

49. Burns, *General Mud*, 221.

50. Falls, slides and flows vary upon the major material present. Except during falls, when rock is the primary material, mud is a principle element during most other landslides.

51. Slim, *Defeat into Victory*, 171–172, 350.

52. Gilmore and Davis, *A Connecticut Yankee in the 8th Gurkha Rifles*, 158.

53. Historical Record: 109th Medical Battalion, RG 407.

54. Slim, *Defeat into Victory*, 340, 344.

55. Sledge, *With the Old Breed*, 248, 260, 233–234.

56. Ibid., 279.

57. Yahara, *The Battle for Okinawa*, 89.

58. Nunneley and Tamayama, *Tales by Japanese Soldiers*, 225.

59. Collins, *Military Geography*, 368. See also 367–385.

60. Ibid., 375–377, 379. The plan meant an invasion of Laos, which was not politically viable and was a significant reason why American forces never implemented OPLAN El Paso.

61. Collins, *Military Geography*, 381, 383.

62. Cobb, Elliott, et al., "Project Popeye Final Report," iv. The name "Project Popeye" was the specific weather modification test conducted against Laos to determine the viability of such an operation. However, this book will use the name Project Popeye when referring to the initial test and the limited operations conducted in Southeast Asia in the late 1960s and early 1970s.

63. Senate Committee, *Weather Modification*, 88–89.
64. Cobb, Elliott, et al., "Project Popeye Final Report," 2.
65. Senate Committee, *Weather Modification*, 88–89.
66. Ibid., 88–89.
67. Frisby, "Weather Modification in Southeast Asia, 1966–1972," 1.
68. Ibid., 4
69. Ibid., 4.
70. Cobb, quoted in Frisby, "Weather Modification in Southeast Asia, 1966–1972," 3.
71. Frisby, "Weather Modification in Southeast Asia, 1966–1972," 4.
72. Cobb, Elliott, et al., "Project Popeye Final Report," iv.
73. Frisby, "Weather Modification in Southeast Asia, 1966–1972," 4.
74. Simons, "Controlling the Weather," September 24, 2001; and Senate Committee, *Weather Modification*, 103, 108, 93.

Chapter 4: Random Mud

1. Von Senger und Etterlin, "March of an Armored Division during the Muddy Season," 104.
2. D'Este, *Patton: A Genius for War*, 686–687, quoted in Collins, *Military Geography*, 69.
3. Horrocks, *A Full Life*, 141.
4. "The Invasion of Russia."
5. Murray and Millett, *A War to Be Won*, 279.
6. Ibid., 297.
7. Glantz and House, *The Battle of Kursk*, 262. July is the rainiest month in the Kursk area, but warm temperatures and dry winds are not conducive to long periods of mud.
8. Glantz and House, *The Battle of Kursk*, 80.
9. Caidin, *The Tigers Are Burning*, 216.
10. Ibid., 176, 165, 198–199.
11. Dunn, *Kursk: Hitler's Gamble*, 146–147.
12. Glantz and House, *The Battle of Kursk*, 164.
13. Dunn, *Kursk: Hitler's Gamble*, 150–151.
14. Glantz and House, *The Battle of Kursk*, 182.
15. Dunn, *Kursk: Hitler's Gamble*, 150.
16. Ibid., 163.
17. Bidermann, *In Deadly Combat*, 84.

18. Carius, *Tigers in the Mud*, 97.
19. Horrocks, *A Full Life*, 246.
20. Horrocks quoted in Elstob, *Battle of the Reichswald*, 7.
21. Elstob, *Battle of the Reichswald*, 89.
22. Ibid., 9, 59.
23. Beale, *Tank Tracks*, 171.
24. Horrocks, *A Full Life*, 249.
25. Beale, *Tank Tracks*, 170.
26. Elstob, *Battle of the Reichswald*, 151, 86–87, 99.
27. Beale, *Tank Tracks*, 176.
28. Horrocks, *A Full Life*, 248–249; and Horrocks quoted in Elstob, *Battle of the Reichswald*, 7.
29. Horrocks quoted in Elstob, *Battle of the Reichswald*, 7.
30. Bidermann, *In Deadly Combat*, 259, 107.
31. Von Senger und Etterlin, "March of an Armored Division during the Muddy Season," 100–101.
32. Bevilacqua, "Operation Killer," 15–16.
33. Grant, *Personal Memoirs of U. S. Grant*, 526, 528.
34. Johnson, *Battlefields of the World War*, 72.
35. Burns, *General Mud*, 154.
36. Dunham, *The Long Carry*, 119.
37. Johnson, *Battlefields of the World War*, 73.
38. Burns, *General Mud*, 72–73.
39. Metelmann, *Through Hell for Hitler*, 67.
40. Chandler, *The Campaigns of Napoleon*, 1061.
41. Bonaparte, *Napoleon's Memoirs*, 515–516.
42. Ibid., 517, 530.
43. Howarth, *A Near Run Thing*, 108.
44. Chandler, *The Campaigns of Napoleon*, 1067.
45. Ibid., 1073.
46. Howarth, *A Near Run Thing*, 89.
47. Chandler, *The Campaigns of Napoleon*, 1080.
48. Howarth, *A Near Run Thing*, 178.
49. Ibid., 116.

Chapter 5: Mud and Engineers

1. The History of the 808th Engineer Aviation Battalion, RG 407.
2. Edwards, "Marco Polo in China, Part II," 38.
3. Sledge, *With the Old Breed*, 190; and Leinbaugh and

Campbell, *The Men of Company K*, 20, 226.

4. Rommel, *Attacks*, 43–44.
5. History, 133rd Infantry, RG 407.
6. Clark, interview.
7. Carius, *Tigers in the Mud*, 176.
8. Herringham, *A Physician in France*, 220–221.
9. Slim, *Defeat into Victory*, 172, 397–398; and Myers, interview.
10. Elstob, *Battle of the Reichswald*, 59.
11. Myers. Warren, et al., eds., *An Informal History of the 631st Field Artillery Battalion*, 70–71.
12. Collins, *Military Geography*, 122; and Rendulic, *Battle in Mud*, 9, 10.
13. Guderian, *Panzer Leader*, 242.
14. Knappe and Brusaw, *Soldat*, 200.
15. Bidermann, *In Deadly Combat*, 158.
16. Ingall, "On Campaign with the Bengal Lancers," 56; and Myers, interview.
17. *The Wipers Times*, 242.
18. Burns, *General Mud*, 57.
19. Sledge, *With the Old Breed*, 261, 262; and Sajer, *The Forgotten Soldier*, 80.
20. Rendulic, *Battle in Mud*, 9.
21. Dunham, *The Long Carry*, 129.
22. Sajer, *The Forgotten Soldier*, 79; and Mauldin, *Up Front*, 39.
23. Action Against Enemy Report, King 2 Operation 1944, 96th Infantry Division, RG 407.
24. Hoffman, "Chesty Puller's Epic Stand," 42.
25. Carius, *Tigers in the Mud*, 101.
26. Hasting and Jenkins, *The Battle for the Falklands*, 279. Trails were the "legs" of towed artillery pieces while the layer was responsible for aiming the weapon.
27. Sledge, *With the Old Breed*, 228–229, 261–262.
28. Action Against Enemy Report, King 2 Operation 1944, 96th Infantry Division, RG 407
29. Ibid.; and Action Report, Ryukyu Campaign, 96th Infantry Division, RG 407.
30. Unit History, 34th Division, RG 407; and Action Against Enemy Report, 321st Engineer Battalion, RG 407.

31. Report of Operations, Headquarters 34th Infantry Division, RG 407.
32. Operations and Intelligence, Periodic Report 321st Engineer Battalion, RG 407.
33. Action Against Enemy Report, 321st Engineer Battalion, RG 407.

Chapter 6: Mud and Morale

1. Burns, *General Mud*, 22.
2. Edelman, ed., *Dear America*, 126.
3. Richardson, *Fighting Spirit*, 171.
4. Holmes, *Firing Line*, 111.
5. Jordan, *Red Diamond Regiment*, 38.
6. Mauldin, *Up Front*, pp. 143–144.
7. Sledge, *With the Old Breed*, 92.
8. Rommel, *Attacks*, 47.
9. Bidermann, *In Deadly Combat*, 97.
10. Grauwin, *Doctor at Dienbienphu*, 228.
11. Dunham, *The Long Carry*, 109.
12. Harry Mielert quoted in Fritz, *Frontsoldaten*, 105.
13. Jones, interview.
14. Johnson, *Battlefields of the World War*, 25.
15. Dunham, *The Long Carry*, 38.
16. Sledge, *With the Old Breed*, 242.
17. Sajer, *The Forgotten Soldier*, 78.
18. Leinbaugh and Campbell, *The Men of Company K*, 220.
19. Stone, "Army Mission Quickly Turns into Quagmire," 3A.
20. Myers, Warren, et al., eds., *An Informal History of the 631st Field Artillery Battalion*, 75.
21. Towne, *Doctor Danger Forward*, 148–149.
22. Owen and Bell, eds., *Wilfred Owen: Collected Letters*, 422. The practice continues among some marines. Desperate to lose "boot" status, some Marines repeatedly washed their camouflage uniforms so they would fade (author's note).
23. Metelmann, *Through Hell for Hitler*, 16.
24. Sassoon, *Memoirs of an Infantry Officer*, 44.
25. Moran, *The Anatomy of Courage*, 78–79; and Kellett, *Combat Motivation*, 242.
26. Simmons, "Stalingrad," 34.
27. Isaacs, "It's a Lovely Day Tomorrow—Burma, 1942–1944."

28. Latimer, "Battle of the Admin Box," 51.
29. Sledge, *With the Old Breed*, 214–215.
30. Jones, interview.
31. Martin and Burton, eds., *A Gentleman and an Officer*, 146.
32. Williams, *From the Cannon's Mouth*, 320–321.
33. Omissi, ed., *Indian Voices of the Great War*, 231, 283.
34. Sledge, *With the Old Breed*, 223–224.
35. Burns, *General Mud*, 130.
36. Sassoon, *Memoirs of an Infantry Officer*, 187, 98.
37. Dunham, *The Long Carry*, 94.
38. Garfield, *The Thousand-Mile War*, 35, 134.
39. Connell, *Wavell*, 242.
40. Owen and Bell, eds., *Wilfred Owen: Collected Letters*, 443.
41. Sledge, *With the Old Breed*, 260.
42. Reilly, *The British at the Gates*, 282.
43. Burns, *General Mud*, 54–55.
44. Myers, interview.
45. The History of the 808th Engineer Aviation Battalion, RG 407.
46. Burns, *General Mud*, 4.
47. Fuchs, *Sieg Heil*, 147.
48. Kellett, *Combat Motivation*, 243.
49. Petre, *Napoleon's Campaign in Poland, 1806–1807*, 95.
50. Dunham, *The Long Carry*, 129.
51. Sledge, *With the Old Breed*, 289.
52. Sajer, *The Forgotten Soldier*, 254–255. Sajer refers to enemy aircraft.
53. Ibid., 269.
54. Nunneley and Tamayama, *Tales by Japanese Soldiers*, 75.
55. Manchester, *Goodbye, Darkness*, 114.
56. Stone, "Army Mission Quickly Turns into Quagmire," 3A.
57. Myers, Warren, et al., eds., *An Informal History of the 631st Field Artillery Battalion*.
58. Report of Operations, Headquarters 34th Infantry Division, RG 407.
59. Leinbaugh and Campbell, *The Men of Company K*, 47.
60. Bombadier J. W. Palmer quoted in Badsey, "The Abomination of Desolation," 268, 269.
61. Metelmann, *Through Hell for Hitler*, 60.
62. Hallas, *Killing Ground on Okinawa*, 31.

63. Burns, *General Mud*, 26.

64. Sledge, *With the Old Breed*, 260.

65. Grauwin, *Doctor at Dienbienphu*, 293.

66. Keegan, *The Face of Battle*, 136.

67. Owen and Bell, eds., *Wilfred Owen: Collected Letters*, 584.

68. Linderman, *The World Within War*, 60.

69. Herringham, *A Physician in France*, 219.

70. Jones, interview.

71. Garfield, *The Thousand-Mile War*, 197.

Chapter 7: Mud and Health

1. Gilbert, *The First World War*, 313.

2. Johnson, *Battlefields of the World War*, 60.

3. Williams, *From the Cannon's Mouth*, 159, 83–84.

4. Winters et al., *Battling the Elements*, 44. Not all of the fifty thousand drowned, but one may surmise that mud was at least responsible for swallowing a significant percentage of the corpses.

5. Remini, *The Battle of New Orleans*, 178.

6. Badsey, "The Abomination of Desolation," 267.

7. Manchester, *Goodbye, Darkness*, 374.

8. Edelman, ed., *Dear America*, 11. Without noting any sources as proof, John Ellis stated on p 45 of *Eye-Deep in Hell* that in November 1916, a British Guards Battalion "lost sixteen men through exhaustion and drowning in mud."

9. Keegan, *The Face of Battle*, 112–113.

10. Root-Bernstein and Root-Bernstein, *Honey, Mud, Maggots*, 101.

11. National Research Council, *Burns, Shock, Wound Healing and Vascular Injuries*, 184.

12. Davis, *Marine*, 150.

13. Koschorrek, *Blood Red Snow*, 237.

14. Grauwin, *Doctor at Dienbienphu*, 83.

15. Lytton, interview. Gas gangrene is "an acute, severe, and painful condition often resulting from dirty, lacerated wounds in which the muscles and subcutaneous tissues become filled with gas and a serosanguineous exudates." (*Dorland's Illustrated Medical Dictionary*)

16. Keegan, *The Face of Battle*, 271, 268; and Ellis, *Eye-Deep in Hell*, 112–113.

17. Grauwin, *Doctor at Dienbienphu*, 269, 59, 182–184, 292. Surprisingly, mud also had positive uses in treating wounds.Until recent medical evidence changed the procedure, mud was an acceptable remedy for retarding the burning of white phosphorous. As the chemical uses oxygen as a source for its continuance, one U.S. Army field manual recommended that soldiers use mud to smother white phosphorous (Department of the Army, *First Aid for Soldiers*, 138).

18. Edelman, ed., *Dear America*, 15.

19. Jones, interview.

20. Sassoon, *Memoirs of an Infantry Officer*, 240.

21. Davis, *Marine,* 146.

22. Grauwin, *Doctor at Dienbienphu*, 159.

23. Lytton, interview.

24. Grauwin, *Doctor at Dienbienphu*, 182–184, 265, 262, 241.

25. Special Action Report, First Marine Division, RG 127.

26. Manchester, *Goodbye, Darkness*, 361.

27. Historical Report for the Year 1944, 796th Ordnance Lt. Maint. Company, RG 407.

28. Root-Bernstein, *Honey, Mud, and Maggots*, 199.

29. Waterman, "Ambushed on the Song Ong Doc."

30. Richards, "Ray Hanson," 55.

31. Collins, *Military Geography,* 88; and Towne, *Doctor Danger Forward,* 147.

32. Collins, *Military Geography*, 88.

33. Herringham, *A Physician in France*, 216–217.

34. Monthly Sanitary Report, Medical Detachment, 133rd Infantry, 34th Division, RG 407.

35. Ellis, *Eye-Deep in Hell*, 48–49.

36. Moran, *The Anatomy of Courage*, 84.

37. Lytton, interview. During his interview, Lytton made it clear that although frostbite and trenchfoot were different ailments, both medical conditions concluded similarly—dead tissue. Therefore, medical officers made their own decisions as to which ailment a soldier suffered. The U.S. Army considered frostbite as an injury received within the line of duty, but trenchfoot was not; hence, medical personnel often gave one diagnoses or the other based on a soldier's character.

38. Unit Reports Nos. 36–51, 381st Infantry, 96th Infantry Division, RG 407.

39. Collins, *Military Geography*, 88–89.

40. Herringham, *A Physician in France*, 217–218. Rubber waders, and thigh and gum boots were other names for this boot type.

41. Dunham, *The Long Carry*, 13, 117.

42. Owen and Bell, eds., *Wilfred Owen: Collected Letters*, 426.

43. Stanton, *U.S. Army Uniforms of World War II*, 254.

44. Lytton, interview. Lytton admitted that he wore the rubber overshoes.

45. Stanton, *U.S. Army Uniforms of the Vietnam War*, 132.

46. Williams, *From the Cannon's Mouth*, 69.

47. McPherson, *Battle Cry of Freedom*, 319.

48. Sorrel, *At the Right Hand of Longstreet*, 133–134.

49. Keegan, *The Face of Battle*, 274, 272–273.

50. Dunham, *The Long Carry*, 19.

51. Slim, *Defeat into Victory*, 349.

52. Gilbert, *The First World War*, 364; and Ellis, *Eye-Deep in Hell*, 107, 109. One stone equals 14 pounds; twelve stone is 168 pounds.

53. Leinbaugh and Campbell, *The Men of Company K*, 65.

54. Dunham, *The Long Carry*, 108.

55. History, 133rd Infantry, RG 407.

56. Sassoon, *Memoirs of an Infantry Officer*, 239.

57. Grant, *Personal Memoirs of U. S. Grant*, 425.

58. Moran, *The Anatomy of Courage*, 129.

59. Barker, *Nightingales in the Mud*, 107.

60. Action Against Enemy Report, King 2 Operation 1944, 96th Infantry Division, RG 407.

61. Action Against the Enemy, 321st Medical Battalion, 96th Infantry Division, RG 407.

62. Ibid.

63. Action Report, Ryukyu Campaign, 96th Infantry Division, RG 407.

64. Special Action Report, First Marine Division, RG 127.

Chapter 8: Mud, Fatigue, Wear and Tear

1. Bidermann, *In Deadly Combat*, 162.

2. Evans and Sasser, *Doc*, 125.

3. Linderman, *The World Within War*, 255–256.

4. McCall, "The Nine-Coordinate Probability Model," Appendix A, 8.

5. Williams, *From the Cannon's Mouth*, 163.
6. Rommel, *Attacks*, 47.
7. Sledge, *With the Old Breed*, 234.
8. Barker, *Nightingales in the Mud*, 107.
9. DiNardo, *Mechanized Juggernaut or Military Anachronism*, 47.
10. Holt, *A Surgeon's Civil War*, 54.
11. Scheel, *Rain, Mud, and Swamps*, 169.10.
12. Sassoon, *Memoirs of an Infantry Officer*, 220–221.
13. Burns, *General Mud*, 58–59.
14. Sledge, *With the Old Breed*, 276–277.
15. Bevilacqua, "Soissons, France 1918," 40.
16. Slim, *Defeat into Victory*, 341.
17. Fuchs, *Sieg Heil,* 147.
18. Turnbull, *The Samurai*, 224.
19. Keegan, *The Face of Battle,* 102; and Jones, *The Art of War in the Western World,* 170.
20. Keegan, *The Face of Battle*, 151.
21. Grant, *Personal Memoirs of U. S. Grant*, 184.
22. Burns, *General Mud*, 18, 20.
23. Gough, *The Fifth Army*, 205; also quoted in Burns, *General Mud*, 54–55.
24. Lt. Gen. Sir Launcelot Kiggell quoted in Winters et al., *Battling the Elements*, 33.
25. Burns, *General Mud*, 22.
26. Grauwin, *Doctor at Dienbienphu*, 259–260.
27. Burns, *General Mud*, 30.
28. Sajer, *The Forgotten Soldier*, 87.
29. Rendulic, *Battle in Mud*, 2.
30. Extract of Journal, 34th Infantry Division, RG 407.
31. Guderian, *Panzer Leader*, 237.
32. Williams, *From the Cannon's Mouth*, 35.
33. History, 133rd Infantry, RG 407.
34. Myers, interview.
35. Ibid.
36. Ibid.
37. Cooper, *Death Traps*, 150.
38. Carius, *Tigers in the Mud*, 121.
39. Myers, interview.
40. Guderian, *Panzer Leader*, 237.
41. Action Against Enemy Report, 381st Infantry, 96th Infantry

Division, RG 407.

42. History, 133rd Infantry, RG 407.

43. Myers, interview.

44. Myers, Warren, et al., eds., *An Informal History of the 631st Field Artillery Battalion,* 73.

45. Dunham, *The Long Carry,* 117; and Johnson, *Battlefields of the World War,* 66.

46. Burns, *General Mud,* 45.

47. After Action Report, 334th Infantry Regiment, RG 407.

48. Johnson, *Battlefields of the World War,* 73, 74.

49. Demaison and Buffetaut, *Honour Bound,* 76, 78–79, 130.

50. Ellis, *Eye-Deep in Hell,* 47.

51. Johnson, *Battlefields of the World War,* 24.

52. Discussion on Sten guns, http://en.wikipedia.org/wiki/Sten

Chapter 9: Forever Mud

1. Squitieri, "What Could Go Wrong," 1A.

2. Hill, "Hydrologic Analysis of Iraq," 16, 17.

3. Livingston, *An Nasiriyah,* 58.

4. Squitieri, "What Could Go Wrong," 1A; and Livingston, *An Nasiriyah,* 90, 59; and Pritchard, *Ambush Alley,* 74–76, 78, 82.

5. Company Commanders, "The Battle of An Nasiriyah," 42; and Livingston, *An Nasiriyah,* 59, 60.

6. Livingston, *An Nasiriyah,* 42, 44, 61, 62, 65.

7. "Up-Armored HMMWV."

8. West and West, "Lessons from Iraq," 112.

9. Frazer, letter.

10. House et al., "Weather as a Force Multiplier," vii; and Wilson, "Weather Wars."

11. House et al., "Weather as a Force Multiplier," 5, 6, 13, 14.

12. Hoeckel, interview, and Christian, "Exclusive SHOT Show Report," 51.

13. Bevilacqua, "Operation Killer," 15–16.

14. Horrocks, *A Full Life,* 249.

15. Beale, *Tank Tracks,* 153.

Appendix

1. Collins, *Military Geography,* 37.

2. Mason, "The Impact of Environment on Military Operations,"

13a, 13b, Table 5, and Table 6. All tables presented are only selected segments of Mason's tables.

3.   Combined arms.

4.   Comfort and hardship also describes this operation.

5.   Mason, "The Impact of Environment on Military Operations," 15a, 15b, Table 7, and Table 8.

BIBLIOGRAPHY

Primary Sources

Unpublished Government Records

Action Against the Enemy, 15 September 1944–25 December 1944, Headquarters 321st Medical Battalion, 96th Infantry Division, World War II Operations Records 1940–48, RG 407, National Archives at College Park.

Action Against Enemy Report, King 2 Operation 1944, 96th Infantry Division, World War II Operations Records 1940–48, RG 407, National Archives at College Park.

Action Against Enemy Report, Okinawa Operation, Ryukyus Campaign, 321st Engineer Battalion, 96th Infantry Division, World War II Operations Records 1940–48, RG 407, National Archives at College Park.

Action Against Enemy Report, Ryukyus Campaign, 1 April 1945–30 June 1945, Headquarters 321st Medical Battalion, 96th Infantry Division, World War II Operations Records 1940–48, RG 407, National Archives at College Park.

Action Against Enemy Report, 381st Infantry, 96th Infantry Division, World War II Operations Records 1940–48, RG 407, National Archives at College Park.

Action Report, Ryukyu Campaign, 96th Infantry Division, World War II Operations Records 1940–48, RG 407, National Archives at College Park.

Activities of the 734th Ordnance Light Maintenance Company, 1–31 December 1944, 34th Infantry Division, World War II Operations Records 1940–48, RG 407, National Archives at College Park.

After Action Report, 18–25 November 1944, 334th Infantry Regiment, 84th Infantry Division, World War II Operations Records 1940–48, RG 407, National Archives at College Park.

After Action Report, December 1944, 84th Quartermaster Company, 84th Infantry Division, World War II Operations Records 1940–48, RG 407, National Archives at College Park.

After Action Report, 1–30 November 1944, 84th Infantry Division, World War II Operations Records 1940–48, RG 407, National Archives at College Park.

Annual Report of Activities, 1944; Medical Detachment 334th Infantry, 84th Infantry Division, World War II Operation Records, 1940–48, National Archives at College Park.

Extract of Journal, 1–31 October 1944; Office of the Division Quartermaster, 34th Infantry Division, World War II Operations Records 1940–48, RG 407, National Archives at College Park.

The History of the 808th Engineer Aviation Battalion, 15 September 1941–12 January 1946; Engineers, World War II Operations Records 1940–48, RG 407, National Archives at College Park.

A History of Machine Shop Truck Unit No. 303, 2nd Division, Records of the American Expeditionary Force (World War I), RG 120, National Archives at College Park.

Historical Record, 109th Medical Battalion, 34th Infantry Division, October 1944, World War II Operations Records 1940–48, RG 407, National Archives at College Park.

Historical Report for the Year 1944, 796th Ordnance Lt. Maint. Company, 96th Infantry Division, World War II Operations Records 1940–48, RG 407, National Archives at College Park.

History, 133rd Infantry, 1 September 1944–30 September 1944, 34th Division, World War II Operations Records 1940–48, RG 407, National Archives at College Park.

History, 133rd Infantry, 1 October 1944–31 October 1944, 34th Division, World War II Operations Records 1940–48, RG 407, National Archives at College Park.

History, 133rd Infantry, 1 December 1944–31 December 1944, 34th Division, World War II Operations Records 1940–48, RG 407, National Archives at College Park.

History, 133rd Infantry, 1 April 1945–3 April 1945, 34th Division, World War II Operations Records 1940–48, RG 407, National Archives at College Park.

History, 133rd Infantry, 1 January 1945–31 January 1945, 34th Division, World War II Operations Records 1940–48, RG 407, National Archives at College Park.

History of the Second Supply Train, Second Division, Records of the American Expeditionary Force (World War I), RG 120, National Archives at College Park.

Monthly Sanitary Report, February 1945, Medical Detachment, 133rd Infantry, 34th Division, World War II Operations Records 1940–48, RG 407, National Archives at College Park.

Narrative of the Action of the 168th Infantry Regiment, 1 October 1943–30 October 1943, 34th Infantry Division, World War II Operations Records 1940–48, RG 407, National Archives at College Park.

Narrative of the Action of the 168th Infantry Regiment, 1 November 1942–30 November 1943, 34th Infantry Division, World War II Operations Records 1940–48, RG 407, National Archives at College Park.

Narrative of the Action of the 168th Infantry Regiment, January 24, 1944–February 29, 1944, 34th Infantry Division, World War II Operations Records 1940–48, RG 407, National Archives at College Park.

Operations and Intelligence Periodic Report, 19 November 1944–17 December 1944, Headquarters 321st Engineer Battalion, 96th Infantry Division, World War II Operations Records 1940 48, RG 407, National Archives at College Park.

Operations Diary, S-3, 817th Engineer Aviation Battalion, World War II Operations Records 1940–48, RG 407, National Archives at College Park.

Report of Operations, Headquarters 34th Infantry Division, United States Army, 1–30 November 1943, World War II

Operations Records 1940–48, RG 407, National Archives at College Park.

Report of Operations, Headquarters 34th Infantry Division, United States Army, 1–31 December 1943, World War II Operations Records 1940–48, RG 407, National Archives at College Park.

Report of Operations, Headquarters 34th Infantry Division, United States Army, 1–31 January 1944, World War II Operations Records 1940–48, RG 407, National Archives at College Park.

Report of Operations, Headquarters 34th Infantry Division, United States Army, 1–30 September 1944, World War II Operations Records 1940–48, RG 407, National Archives at College Park.

Report of Operations, Headquarters 34th Infantry Division, United States Army, 1–31 October 1944, World War II Operations Records 1940–48, Record Group 407, National Archives at College Park.

Report of Operations, Headquarters 34th Infantry Division, United States Army, 1–31 December 1944, World War II Operations Records 1940–48, RG 407, National Archives at College Park.

Report of Operations, Headquarters 34th Infantry Division, United States Army, 1–31 January 1945, World War II Operations Records 1940–48, RG 407, National Archives at College Park.

Report of Operations, Headquarters 34th Infantry Division, United States Army, 1–28 February 1945, World War II Operations Records 1940–48, RG 407, National Archives at College Park.

S-3 Journal, May 1945, Fifth Marine Regiment; Records Relating to U.S. Marine Corps Operations in World War II (Geographic Files) Okinawa, RG 127, National Archives at College Park.

S-3 Periodic Report, Headquarters First Battalion, 135th Infantry, CCA, First Armored Division, World War II Operations Records 1940–48, RG 407, National Archives at College Park.

Special Action Report, Okinawa Nansei-Shoto, 1945, First Marine Division (Rein), Records Relating to United States Marine Corps Operations in World War II (Geographic Files) Okinawa, RG 127, National Archives at College Park.

Unit History, 34th Division CG, G-1, G-2, G-3, G-4, Sections 1–31 October 1944, 34th Division, World War II Operations Records 1940–48, RG 407, National Archives at College Park.

Unit Journals, To Accompany Action Against Enemy Report, Okinawa Operation, April 1, 1945–June 30, 1945 First and Third Battalions RCT 381, 96th Infantry Division, World War II Operations Records 1940–48, RG 407, National Archives at College Park.

Unit Reports No. 36–51, 381st Infantry (Reinf), 21 May 1945–6 June 1945, 96th Infantry Division, World War II Operations Records 1940–48, RG 407, National Archives at College Park.

Published Government Records

Baker, Robert F. "Landslide Treatment in the Theater of Operations." Progress Report No. 3 on Project No. CE-134. Columbus, Ohio: 2701st USAR Research and Development Unit (Reinf-Tng.), 1958.

Campbell, Robert D. "The Environmental Element in Military Operations." Historical Records Project, Final Report: Section 2. Washington, D.C.: George Washington Univ., 1957.

Cobb, James T., Jr., Shelden D. Elliott, Jr., and others. "Project Popeye Final Report." China Lake, Calif.: Naval Weapons Center, 1967.

Hesaltine, Charles Edwin, Jr. "Military Operations as Characterized by Terrain." Historical Records Project, Final Report: Section 3. Washington, D.C.: George Washington Univ., 1957.

Hill, Randall R. "Earth and Water Make More Than Mud." Fort Leavenworth, Kans.: School of Advanced Military Studies, U.S. Army Command and General Staff College, 1989.

Mason, Norman Randolph, Jr. "The Impact of Environment on Military Operations." Historical Records Project, Final Report: Section 4. Washington, D.C.: George Washington Univ., 1957.

McCall, Chester H., Jr. "The Nine-Coordinate Probability Model Describing Environment-Military Operations Relationships." Historical Records Project, Final Report: Section 5. Washington, D.C.: George Washington Univ., 1957.

Myers, Allan L., Donald C. Warren, and others, eds. *An Informal History of the 631st Field Artillery Battalion.*

National Research Council, Committee on Surgery of the Division of Medical Sciences. *Burns, Shock, Wound Healing and Vascular Injuries.* Military Surgical Manuals Vol. 5. Philadelphia: W. B. Saunders, 1943.

Rendulic, Lothar. *Battle in Mud.* Edited by L. Schaefer. Translated by A. Rosenwald. Historical Division, European Command. Washington, D.C.: Government Printing Office, 1951.

Strahler, Arthur N., and Koons Donaldson. "Objective and Quantitative Field Methods of Terrain Analysis." Final Report of Project NR 387-021. New York: Columbia Univ., 1960.

Thornthwaite, C. W. "Estimating Soil Tractionability by Climatic Analysis." Environmental Protection Section Report No. 167. Seabrook, N.J.: John Hopkins Univ. Laboratory of Climatology, 1950.

U.S. Department of the Army. "Beat the Mud Handbook: Expedient Field Guide to Surviving the Spring Thaw." Vicksburg, Miss.: U.S. Army Waterways Experiment Station, 1996.

_____. *Combat in Russian Forests and Swamps.* German Report Series. No. 20-231. July 1951.

_____. *First Aid for Soldiers.* Field Manual. FM 21-11. June 1976.

_____. *Military Improvisations during the Russian Campaign.* German Report Series. No. 20-201. August 1951.

_____. *Terrain Analysis.* FM 5-33. July 1990.

_____. *Terrain Factors in the Russian Campaign.* German Report Series. No. 20-290. July 1951.

_____. Corps of Engineers. "Trafficability of Soils: Trafficability Studies—Fort Churchill." Technical Memorandum No. 3-240, Second Supplement. Vicksburg, Miss., 1948.

_____. Corps of Engineers. "Trafficability of Soils: Vehicle Classification." Technical Memorandum No. 3-240, Ninth Supplement. Vicksburg, Miss., 1951.

U.S. Department of the Navy, U.S. Marine Corps. *Small Unit Leader's Guide to Weather and Terrain.* OH 0-51. August 1990.

U.S. Senate Committee on Foreign Relations. *Weather Modification: Hearings before the Subcommittee on Oceans and International Environment.* 93rd Cong., 2nd sess., March 20, 1974.

U.S. War Department. "Low Pressure Tires in Mud." Report No. 796. Fort Belvoir, Va.: U.S. Army Corps of Engineers, 1944.

Newspapers

Leiby, Richard. "In Kuwait City, the Calm before a Mud Storm: With the Threatened War Looming, Citizens Try to Stay Cool, and Dry." *Washington Post,* March 11, 2003.

Lynch, David J. "In Nasiriyah, a Surreal Battle." *USA Today,* March 28, 2003.

Lynch, David, Steven Komarow, and Gregg Zoroya. "Storms Halt Helicopters and Convoys." *USA Today,* March 26, 2003.

Simons, Paul. "Controlling the Weather." Special Report: The Weather. *The Guardian,* September 24, 2001.

Squitieri, Tom. "What Could Go Wrong." *USA Today,* March 13, 2003.

Stone, Andrea. "Army Mission Quickly Turns into Quagmire." *USA Today,* April 20, 1999.

The Wipers Times: A Complete Facsimile of the Famous World War One Trench Newspaper, Incorporating the "New Church" Times, The Kemmel Times, The Somme Times, The B.E.F. Times, and the "Better Times." London: Peter Davies, 1973.

Books

Beale, Peter. *Tank Tracks: 9th Battalion Royal Tank Regiment at War 1940–45*. Phoenix Mill Stroud, U.K.: Budding Books, 1995.

Bidermann, Gottlob Herbert. *In Deadly Combat: A German Soldier's Memoir of the Eastern Front*. Translated and edited by Derek S. Zumbro. Lawrence: Univ. Press of Kansas, 2000.

Bonaparte, Napoleon. *Napoleon's Memoirs*. Edited by Somerset De Chair. London: Faber & Faber, 1948.

Burns, E. L. M. *General Mud: Memoirs of Two World Wars*. Toronto: Clarke, Irwin, 1970.

Carius, Otto. *Tigers in the Mud*. Translated by Robert J. Edwards. Winnipeg, M.B.: J. J. Fedorowicz Publishing, 1992.

Catanzaro, Francis B. *With the 41st Division in the Southwest Pacific: A Foot Soldier's Story*. Indianapolis: Indiana Univ. Press, 2002.

Congressional Medal of Honor Library: Vietnam—The Names, the Deeds. New York: Dell Publishing, 1984.

Conroy, Jason. *Heavy Metal: A Tank Company's Battle to Baghdad*. With Ron Martz. Washington, D.C.: Potomac Books, Inc., 2005.

Cooper, Belton Y. *Death Traps: The Survival of an American Armored Division in World War II*. Novato, Calif: Presidio Press, 1998.

Dunham, Frank. *The Long Carry: The Journal of Stretcher Bearer Frank Dunham, 1916–18*. Edited by R. H. Haigh and P. W. Turner. New York: Pergamon Press, 1970.

Edelman, Bernard, ed. *Dear America: Letters Home from Vietnam*. New York: Simon & Schuster, 1985.

Evans, Daniel E., Jr., and Charles W. Sasser. *Doc: Platoon Medic*. New York: Simon & Schuster, 1998.

Fuchs, Karl. *Sieg Heil! War Letters of Tank Gunner Karl Fuchs, 1937–1941*. Compiled, edited, and translated by Horst Fuchs Richardson. North Haven, Conn.: Archon Books, 1987.

Gilmore, Scott, and Patrick Davis. *A Connecticut Yankee in the 8th Gurkha Rifles: A Burma Memoir*. Washington, D.C.: Brassey's, Inc., 1995.

Gough, Hubert. *The Fifth Army*. London: Hodder and Stoughton, 1931.

_____. *Soldiering On*: *Being the Memoirs of General Sir Hubert Gough*. New York: Speller and Sons, 1957.

Grant, Ulysses S. *Personal Memoirs of U. S. Grant*. Edited by E. B. Long. New York: C. L. Webster, 1885–86; Bartleby.com, 2000.

Grauwin, Paul. *Doctor at Dienbienphu*.Translated by James Oliver. New York: John Day, 1955.

Graves, Robert. *Complete Poems Volume 1*. Edited by Beryl Graves and Dunstan Ward. Manchester, U.K.: Carcanet Press, 1995.

_____. *Good-bye to All That*. Reprint, New York: Doubleday, 1998.

Grossjohann, Georg. *Five Years, Four Fronts: The War Years of Georg Grossjohann*. Translated by Ulrich Abele. Bedford, Penn.: Aberjona Press, 1999.

Guderian, Heinz. *Panzer Leader*. Translated by Constantine Fitzgibbon. Reprint, Cambridge, Mass.: DaCapo Press, 1996.

Hallock, Judith Lee, ed. *The Civil War Letters of Joshua K. Callaway*. Athens: Univ. of Georgia Press, 1997.

Hennel, George. *A Gentleman Volunteer: The Letters of George Hennel from the Peninsular War, 1812–1813*. Edited by Michael Glover. London: William Heinemann, 1979.

Herringham, Wilmot. *A Physician in France*. London: Edward Arnold, 1919.

Hoess, Rudolf. *Commandant of Auschwitz: The Autobiography of Rudolf Hoess*. Translated by Constantine FitzGibbon. Reprint, London: Phoenix Press, 1995.

Holt, Daniel M. *A Surgeon's Civil War: The Letters and Diary of Daniel M. Holt, M.D.* Edited by James M. Greiner, Janet L. Coryell, and James R. Smither. Kent, Ohio: Kent State Univ. Press, 1994.

Horrocks, Brian. *A Full Life*. London: Collins, 1960.

Kitching, George. *Mud and Green Fields: The Memoirs of Major-General George Kitching*. St. Catharines, Ont.: Vanwell Publishing, 1993.

Knappe, Siegfried, and Ted Brusaw. *Soldat: Reflections of a German Soldier, 1936–1949*. New York: Orion Books, 1992.

Koschorrek, Günter K. *Blood Red Snow: The Memoirs of a German Soldier on the Eastern Front*. Translated by Olav R. Crone-Aamot. London: Greenhill Books, 2002.

Leinbaugh, Harold P., and John D. Campbell. *The Men of Company K: The Autobiography of a World War II Rifle Company*. New York: William Morrow, 1985.

Luck, Hans von. *Panzer Commander: The Memoirs of Colonel Hans von Luck*. New York: Dell Publishing, 1989.

MacDonald, Charles B. *Company Commander*. Reprint, New York: Bantam Books, 1978.

Manchester, William. *Goodbye, Darkness*. Boston: Little, Brown, 1979.

Mauldin, Bill. *Mauldin's Army*. Reprint, Novato, Calif.: Presidio Press, 1983.

_____. *Up Front*. Reprint, New York: Henry Holt, 1968.

McArthur, Judith N., and Orville Vernon Burton, eds. *A Gentleman and an Officer: A Military and Social History of James B. Griffin's Civil War*. New York: Oxford Univ. Press, 1996.

Metelmann, Henry. *Through Hell for Hitler: A Dramatic First-hand Account of Fighting on the Eastern Front with the Wehrmacht*. Havertown, Penn.: Casemate, 1990.

Michaels, G. J. *Tip of the Spear: U.S. Marine Light Armor in the Gulf War*. Annapolis, Md.: Naval Institute Press, 1998.

Miller, Walter H. *Diary of a Yankee Doughboy in World War I: A Story of Bombs, Shells, Mud, Rats and God*. Portland, Maine: Seavey Printers, 1975.

Montgomery, Bernard Law. *The Memoirs of Field-Marshal the Viscount Montgomery of Alamein, K.G.* Cleveland: World Publishing, 1958.

Moran, Lord. *The Anatomy of Courage*. Boston: Houghton Mifflin, 1967.

Muehrcke, Robert C., ed. *Orchids in the Mud: Personal Accounts by Veterans of the 132rd Infantry Regiment*. Chicago: J. S. Printing, 1985.

Nunneley, John, and Kazuo Tamayama. *Tales by Japanese Soldiers: Of the Burma Campaign 1942–1945*. London: Cassell, 2000.

Omissi, David, ed. *Indian Voices of the Great War: Soldiers' Letters, 1914–18*. New York: St. Martin's Press, 1999.

Owen, Harold, and John Bell, eds. *Wilfred Owen: Collected Letters*. New York: Oxford Univ. Press, 1967.

Owen, Wilfred. *War Poems and Others*. Edited by Dominic Hibberd. London: Chatto & Windus, 1973.

Raus, Erhard. *Panzers on the Eastern Front: General Erhard Raus and his Panzer Divisions in Russia, 1941–1945*. Edited by Peter G. Tsouras. Mechanicsburg, Penn.: Lionel Leventhal, 2002.

Rommel, Erwin. *Attacks*. Provo, Utah: Athena Press, 1979.

Sajer, Guy. *The Forgotten Soldier*. Reprint, Washington, D.C.: Brassey's, Inc., 1990.

Sakurai, Tadayoshi. *Human Bullets: A Soldier's Story of the Russo-Japanese War*. Reprint, with introduction by Roger J. Spiller. Lincoln: Univ. of Nebraska Press Bison Books, 1999.

Sassoon, Siegfried. *Collected Poems 1908–1956*. London: Faber & Faber, 1961.

———. *Memoirs of an Infantry Officer*. London: Faber & Faber, 1930.

Senger und Etterlin, Frido von. *Neither Fear Nor Hope*. London: Macdonald, 1963.

Shipp, John. *The Path of Glory: Being the Memoirs of the Extraordinary Career of John Shipp Written by Himself*. Edited by C. J. Stranks. London: Chatto & Windus, 1969.

Sledge, E. B. *With the Old Breed: At Peleliu and Okinawa*. Reprint, New York: Oxford Univ. Press, 1990.

Slim, William. *Defeat into Victory*. London: Cassell, 1956.

Sorrel, G. Moxley. *At the Right Hand of Longstreet: Recollections of a Confederate Staff Officer*. Reprint with introduction by Peter S. Carmichael. Lincoln: Univ. of Nebraska Press, 1999.

Strong, Kenneth. *Intelligence at the Top: The Recollections of an Intelligence Officer*. Garden City, N.Y.: Doubleday, 1969.

Sun-tzu. *The Art of War*. Translated by Samuel B. Griffith. Reprint with foreword by B. H. Liddell Hart. New York: Oxford Univ. Press, 1982.

Towne, Allen N. *Doctor Danger Forward: A World War II Memoir of a Combat Medical Aidman, First Infantry Division*. Jefferson, N.C.: McFarland, 2000.

Walter, Jakob. *The Diary of a Napoleonic Foot Soldier*. Edited by Mark Raeff. Translated from *Denkwurdige Geshichtschreibung über die erlebte Militäridienstzeit des Verfassers dieses Schreibens*. New York: Doubleday, 1991.

Williams, Alpheus S. *From the Cannon's Mouth: The Civil War Letters of General Alpheus S. Williams*. Edited by Milo M. Quaife. Reprint with introduction by Gary W. Gallagher. Lincoln: Univ. of Nebraska Press, 1995.

Yahara, Hiromichi. *The Battle for Okinawa*. Translated by Roger Pineau and Masatoshi Uehara. New York: Wiley and Sons, 1995.

Articles

Castelletto, Alberto. "The Last Horse Warriors." Translated by Philip Monteleoni. *World War II*, January 2004.

Company Commanders, First Battalion, Second Marines. "The Battle of An Nasiriyah." *Marine Corps Gazette*, September 2003.

Doolittle, James. "Jimmy Doolittle: The Man Behind the Legend." Interview by Colin D. Heaton. *World War II*, March 2003.

Eby, Jeffrey L. "A Marine Gunner's View." *Marine Corps Gazette*, October 2003.

Ingall, Francis. "On Campaign with the Bengal Lancers." Interview by Eric Niderost. *World War II*, November 2002.

Jennewein, Hans. "Survival in the Wilderness." Interview by Colin D. Heaton. *World War II*, December 2004.

Mallonee, Gordon Lee. "One Man's War." *World War II*, September 2004.

Pentecost, Thomas J. "A Combat View from the Point." *Marine Corps Gazette*, October 2003.

Simpson, Ross W. "Road to Baghdad." *Leatherneck*, September 2003.

Waterman, Steven L. "Ambushed on the Song Ong Doc." www.justasailor.com/songongdoc.html. Originally published as "Ruff Puff Rambos." *Soldier of Fortune Magazine*, November 1994.

Interviews

Clark, Danny. Nebraska Army National Guard. Interview by author. Tape recording, April 11, 1997, Lincoln, Nebr.

Hamric, Rexile. Interview by author. August 4, 2005, Glenville, W.Va.

Hoeckel, Kristen. Interview by author. May 28, 2005, New River, W.Va.

Jones, Matt. Interview by author. Tape recording, April 22, 2002, Lincoln, Nebr.

Lytton, George. Interview by author. Tape recording, April 25, 2002, Lincoln, Nebr.

Myers, Ivyl Lamar. Interview by author. Tape recording, June 6, 2001, Urbandale, Iowa.

Secondary Sources

Books

Barker, Marianne. *Nightingales in the Mud: The Digger Sisters of the Great War, 1914–1918.* Boston: Allen & Unwin, 1989.

Baynes, John. *Morale: A Study of Men and Courage.* New York: Praeger, 1967.

Beevor, Antony. *The Spanish Civil War.* New York: Bedrick Books, 1982.

Bryant, Anthony. *Sekigahara 1600: The Final Struggle for Power*. Osprey Military Campaign Series 40. Toronto: Reed International Books, 1995.

Caidin, Martin. *The Tigers Are Burning*. New York: Hawthorn Books, 1974.

Cerasini, Marc A. *Heroes: Marine Corps Medal of Honor Winners*. New York: Berkley Publishing, 2002.

Chandler, David. *The Campaigns of Napoleon*. New York: MacMillan, 1966.

Collins, James L., Jr., ed. *The Marshall Cavendish Illustrated Encyclopedia of World War II*. Vol. 6. New York: Cavendish, 1972.

Collins, John M. *Military Geography: For Professionals and the Public*. Reprint, Washington, D.C.: Brassey's, Inc., 1998.

Connell, John. *Wavell: Scholar and Soldier, To June 1941*. London: Collins, 1964.

Davis, Burke. *Marine! The Life of Lt. Gen. Lewis B. (Chesty) Puller, USMC (Ret.)*. Reprint, New York: Bantam Books, 1964.

Demaison, Gerard, and Yves Buffetaut. *Honour Bound: The Chauchat Machine Rifle*. Edited by R. Blake Stevens. Cobourg, Ont.: Collector Grade Publications, 1995.

D'Este, Carlo. *Patton: A Genius for War*. New York: HarperCollins, 1995.

DiNardo, R. L. *Mechanized Juggernaut or Military Anachronism? Horses and the German Army of World War II*. New York: Greenwood Press, 1991.

Dorland's Illustrated Medical Dictionary, 27th ed. Philadelphia: W. B. Saunders, 1988.

Dunn, Walter S., Jr. *Kursk: Hitler's Gamble, 1943*. Westport, Conn.: Praeger, 1997.

Eggenberger, David. *A Dictionary of Battles*. New York: Crowell, 1967.

Ellis, John. *Eye-Deep in Hell: Trench Warfare in World War I*. Reprint, Baltimore: John Hopkins Univ. Press, 1989.

Elstob, Peter. *Battle of the Reichswald*. Ballantine's Illustrated History of World War II. New York: Ballantine Books, 1970.

Fay, Peter Ward. *The Opium War: 1840–1842*. Chapel Hill: Univ. of North Carolina Press, 1975.

Fritz, Stephen G. *Frontsoldaten: The German Soldier in World War II*. Lexington: Univ. of Kentucky Press, 1995.

Garfield, Brian. *The Thousand-Mile War: World War II in Alaska and the Aleutians*. Reprint, New York: Bantam Books, 1982.

Gilbert, Martin. *The First World War: A Complete History*. New York: Henry Holt, 1994.

Glantz, David M., and Jonathan M. House. *The Battle of Kursk*. Lawrence: Univ. of Kansas Press, 1999.

_____. *When Titans Clashed: How the Red Army Stopped Hitler*. Lawrence: Univ. Press of Kansas, 1995.

Gregory, Herbert E., ed. *Military Geology and Topography*. New Haven, Conn.: Yale Univ. Press, 1918.

Hallas, James H. *Killing Ground on Okinawa: The Battle for Sugar Loaf Hill*. Westport, Conn.: Praeger, 1996.

Hasting, Max, and Simon Jenkins. *The Battle for the Falklands*. London: Pan Books, 1983.

Hibbert, Christopher. *Cavaliers and Roundheads*. New York: Charles Scribner's Sons, 1993.

_____. *The Great Mutiny; India 1857*. New York: Viking Press, 1978.

_____. *Wolfe at Quebec*. New York: World Publishing, 1959.

Holmes, Richard. *Firing Line*. London: Jonathon Cape, 1985.

Howard, Michael. *The Franco-Prussian War: The German Invasion of France, 1870–1871*. New York: MacMillan, 1962.

Howarth, David. *A Near Run Thing: The Day of Waterloo*. London: Collins, 1968.

Johnson, Douglas W. *Battlefields of the World War, Western and Southern Fronts: A Study in Military Geography*. New York: Oxford Univ. Press, 1921.

Jones, Archer. *The Art of War in the Western World*. New York: Oxford Univ. Press, 1987.

Jordan, William B. *Red Diamond Regiment: The 17th Maine Infantry*. Shippensburg, Penn.: White Mane Publishing, 1996.

Keegan, John, ed. *Churchill's Generals*. New York: Grove Weidenfeld, 1991.

_____. *The Face of Battle: A Study of Agincourt, Waterloo, and the Somme*. Reprint, New York: Viking Penguin, 1986.

Kellett, Anthony. *Combat Motivation: The Behavior of Soldiers in Battle*. International Series in Management Science/ Operations Research, ser. ed. James P. Ignizio. Boston: Kluwer, 1982.

Laffin, John. *Jack Tar: The Story of the British Sailor*. London: Cassell, 1969.

Linderman, Gerald F. *The World Within War: America's Combat Experience in World War II*. New York: Free Press, 1997.

Livingston, Gary. *An Nasiriyah: The Fight for the Bridges*. North Topsail Island, N.C.: Caisson Press, 2003.

Markey, Joseph I. *From Iowa to the Philippines: A History of Company M, Fifty-first Iowa Infantry Volunteers*. Red Oak, Iowa: Murphy, 1900.

McPherson, James M. *Battle Cry of Freedom: The Era of the Civil War*. Oxford: Oxford University Press, 1988.

Monkhouse, F. J. *A Dictionary of Geography*. Reprint, London: Edward Arnold, 1970.

Moore, W. G. *A Dictionary of Geography*. Reprint, Baltimore: Penguin Books, 1968.

Morgan, David. *The Mongols*. New York: Basil Blackwell, 1986.

Murray, Williamson, and Allan R. Millett. *A War to Be Won: Fighting the Second World War*. Cambridge, Mass.: Belknap Press of Harvard Univ. Press, 2000.

Nicholson, G. W. L. *The Canadians in Italy, 1943–1945*. Official History of the Canadian Army in the Second World War Volume II. Ottawa: Minister of National Defense, 1957.

Ogburn, Charlton, Jr. *The Marauders*. New York: Harper Brothers, 1956.

O'Sullivan, Patrick. *Terrain and Tactics*. New York: Greenwood Press, 1991.

O'Sullivan, Patrick, and Jesse W. Miller. *The Geography of Warfare*. New York: St. Martin's Press, 1983.

Peltier, Louis C., comp. *Bibliography of Military Geography*. Princeton, N.J.: Military Geography Committee,

Association of American Geographers, 1962.

Peltier, Louis C., and G. Etzel Pearcy. *Military Geography*. New York: Norstrand, 1966.

Petre, F. Loraine. *Napoleon's Campaign in Poland, 1806–1807: A Military History of Napoleon's First War with Russia*. New York: Lane, 1907.

Pritchard, Tim. *Ambush Alley: The Most Extraordinary Battle of the Iraq War*. New York: Ballantine Books, 2005.

Reilly, Robin. *The British at the Gates: The New Orleans Campaign in the War of 1812*. New York: Putnam, 1974.

Remini, Robert V. *The Battle of New Orleans*. New York: Penguin Books, 1999.

Richardson, F. M. *Fighting Spirit: A Study of Psychological Factors in War*. New York: Crane, Russak, 1978.

Root-Bernstein, Robert, and Michèle Root-Bernstein. *Honey, Mud, Maggots, and Other Medical Marvels: The Science Behind Folk Remedies and Old Wives' Tales*. Boston: Houghton Mifflin, 1997.

Scheel, Gary L. *Rain, Mud, and Swamps: 31st Missouri Volunteer Infantry Regiment Marching through the South during the Civil War with General William T. Sherman*. Saint Louis: Plus Communications, 1998.

Spence, Jonathon D. *God's Chinese Son: The Taiping Heavenly Kingdom of Hong Xiuquan*. New York: W. W. Norton, 1996.

Spiller, Roger. ed. *Combined Arms in Battle since 1939*. Fort Leavenworth, Kans.: U.S. Army Command and General Staff College Press, 1992.

Stamp, Dudley L., ed. *A Glossary of Geographical Terms*. Reprint, London: Longmans, Green, 1968.

Stanton, Shelby. *U.S. Army Uniforms of the Korean War*. Harrisburg, Penn.: Stackpole Books, 1992.

_____. *U.S. Army Uniforms of the Vietnam War*. Harrisburg, Penn.: Stackpole Books, 1989.

_____. *U.S. Army Uniforms of World War II*. Harrisburg, Penn.: Stackpole Books, 1991.

Strahler, Alan, and Arthur Strahler. *Introducing Physical Geography*. 3rd ed. New York: Wiley and Sons, 2003.

Swinson, Arthur. *The Battle of Kohima*. Great Battles of the Modern World Series. New York: Stein and Day, 1966.

Thucydides. *The Peloponnesian War*. Translated with an introduction by Rex Warner. Reprint, Baltimore: Penguin Books, 1961.

Turnbull, S. R. *The Samurai: A Military History*. Reprint, London: Osprey Publishing, 1983.

Winters, Harold A., Gerald E. Galloway Jr., William J. Reynolds, and David W. Rhyne. *Battling the Elements: Weather and Terrain in the Conduct of War*. Baltimore: John Hopkins Univ. Press, 1998.

Articles

Astor, Gerald. "Victory in Defeat." *World War II*, December 2004.

Badsey, Stephen. "The Abomination of Desolation: Passchendaele, Belgium, 1917." In *Battlegrounds: Geography and the History of Warfare*. Edited by Michael Stephenson. Washington, D.C.: National Geographic, 2003.

_____. "They Shall Not Pass: Verdun, France, 1916." In *Battlegrounds: Geography and the History of Warfare*. Edited by Michael Stephenson. Washington, D.C.: National Geographic, 2003.

Bevilacqua, Allan C. "Operation Killer." *Leatherneck*, March 2001.

_____. "Operation Mixmaster." *Leatherneck*, March 2002.

_____. "Operation Ripper." *Leatherneck*, April 2001.

_____. "The Raid on Ungok." Series: Korea. *Leatherneck*, February 2003.

_____. "Soissons, France 1918." *Leatherneck*, November 2001.

Camp, Dick, Jr. "Remembrances: The Siege of Khe Sanh, 1968." *Leatherneck*, March 2003.

Christian, Jack. "Exclusive SHOT Show Report: Off-the Shelf Outdoor Products Available to All Marines." *Leatherneck*, April 2003.

Drea, Ed. "A Very Savage Operation." *World War II*, September 2002.

Dyck, Ludwig Heinrich. "Operation Goodwood." *World War II*, July/August 2004.

Edwards, Mike."Marco Polo in China, Part II." *National Geographic*, June 2001.

Fleming, Thomas."New Orleans: The Battle That Saved America." *MHQ: The Quarterly Journal of Military History*, Winter 2001.

Frisby, E. M. "Weather Modification in Southeast Asia, 1966–1972." *The Journal of Weather Modification*, April 1982.

Graham, Martin F. "High Tide at Bastogne." *World War II*, December 2004.

Guttman, Jon. "Closing the Falaise Pocket." *World War II*, September 2001.

_____. "South Africa's Armored Cars." *World War II*, November 2004.

Hemingway, Al. "Tangle in Ia Drang Valley." *VFW*, November 2003.

Hill, James R. "Hydrologic Analysis of Iraq for Operation IRAQI FREEDOM." *Marine Corps Gazette*, February 2005.

Hoffman, Jon T. "Chesty Puller's Epic Stand." *World War II*, November 2002.

House, Tamzy J., and others. "Weather as a Force Multiplier: Owning the Weather in 2025." August 1996. research.au. af.mil/papers/ay1996/spacecast/vol3ch15.pdf.

Keene, R. R. "Where Even Monkeys Fall from Trees." *Leatherneck*, January 2002.

Kennedy, Stephen J. and Alice F. Park. "The Army Green Uniform." Technical Report 68-41-CM. Series: C&OM-43. Natick, Mass.:U.S. Army Natick Laboratories, 1968. www.qm found.com/Army_Green_Uniform.htm

Latimer, Jon. "Battle of the Admin Box." *World War II*, December 2004.

Lippman, David H. "The Tiger of Malaya." *World War II*, March 2003.

Lochet, Jean. "On Mud: Artillery, Cavalry, Infantry and the Napoleonic Roads." *Empires Eagles and Lions*, August 1994.

Lochet, Jean, and Jean-Philippe Saujet. "The Six Days: Part I of the 1814 Campaign in France." Illustrations by Keith Rocco. *Empires Eagles and Lions*, August 1994.

Lochet, Jean, Jean-Philippe Saujet, and George Nafziger. "The Battle of Montmirail: Part III of the Six Days Campaign of the 1814 Campaign in France." *Empires Eagles and Lions*, November-December 1994.

Maestre, Ruben D. "The Lance Corporal Who Ensured No Marine Was Left Behind. *Leatherneck*, June 2004.

McManus, John. "Bloody Cisterna." *World War II*, January 2004.

O'Brien, Michael R. "Hut! Two! Three!" *World War II*, January 2004.

Rabinovich, Abraham. "Assault across the Suez." *Military History Quarterly*, Winter 2005.

Richards, James J. "Ray Hanson: Fighting Leatherneck and Football Legend." *Leatherneck*, January 2002.

Senger und Etterlin, F. M. von. "March of an Armored Division during the Muddy Season." *Military Review*, September 1955. Translated from *Wehrkunde*, March 1955.

Showalter, Dennis. "Operation Barbarossa: Hitler's Greatest Gambit." *World War II*, May 2001.

Simmons, Edwin Howard. "Coping with the COLD at Chosin." *Leatherneck*, December 2001.

———. "Stalingrad." *World War II*, January 2003.

Smith, Robert Barr. "The Chindits Heroic Sacrifice at Blackpool." *World War II*. May 2001.

———. "The Greatest Raid of All." *World War II*, March 2003.

Talbot, Randy. "A Bond of Brotherhood." *Leatherneck*, February 2003.

Trudeau, Noah Andre. "Prussia's American Observers." *Military History Quarterly*, Winter 2005.

"Up-Armored HMMWV." August 2005. www.globalsecurity.org/military/systems/ground/hmmwvua.htm.

Weed, Susun S. "Ease Those Bug Bites with Easy Herbs." 2000. www.susunweed.com/Article_Bug Bites.htm.

West, F. J., and Owen West. "Lessons from Iraq." *Popular Mechanics*, August 2005.

West, F. J., and Ray L. Smith. "Implications from Operation Iraqi FREEDOM for the Marine Corps." *Marine Corps Gazette*, November 2003.

Wilson, Jim. "Weather Wars." *Popular Mechanics*, February 1997. www.popularmechanics.com/science/military/1997/2/ weather_wars.

Documentaries

"Alexander vs. Von Arnim." *Clash of Warriors*. History Channel, September 23, 2001.

Burns, John. *News Hour with Jim Lehrer*. March 26, 2003.

Burns, Ken. "1863: Simply Murder." *The Civil War*. Videocassette. Produced by Ken Burns and Ric Burns. Time-Life Video, 1990.

"The Invasion of Italy." *Battlefield*. Nebraska Educational Television, April 14, 2002.

"The Invasion of Russia." *Battlefield*. Nebraska Educational Television, April 12, 2002.

Isaacs, Jeremy. "Barbarossa, June–December 1941." *The World at War*. Videocassette. Produced by Peter Batty. Thames Television, 1973, 1974.

_____. "The Desert North Africa, 1940–1943." *The World at War*. Videocassette. Produced by Peter Batty. Thames Television, 1973, 1974.

_____. "It's a Lovely Day Tomorrow—Burma, 1942–1944." *The World at War*. Videocassette. Produced by John Pett. Thames Television 1973, 1974.

_____. "Remember." *The World at War*. Videocassette. Produced by Jeremy Isaacs. Thames Television, 1973, 1974.

_____. "Tough Old Gut—Italy, November 1942–June 1944." *The World at War*. Videocassette. Produced by Ben Shepard. Thames Television, 1973, 1974.

Klein, Larry. "Matters of Life and Death." *A Science Odyssey: The Journal of a Century*. Videocassette. WGBH Educational Foundation, 1998.

Letter

Frazer, William, letter to author, July 1, 2005.

INDEX